Blind Boone

Project Sponsors

Missouri Center for the Book, Jefferson City

Western Historical Manuscript Collection, University of
  Missouri–Columbia

Special Thanks

A. E. Schroeder

Fae Sotham, State Historical Society of Missouri, Columbia

Paul Szopa, Academic Support Center, University of
  Missouri–Columbia

Missouri Heritage Readers

General Editor,

Rebecca B. Schroeder

Each Missouri Heritage Reader explores a particular aspect of the state's rich cultural heritage. Focusing on people, places, historical events, and the details of daily life, these books illustrate the ways in which people from all parts of the world contributed to the development of the state and the region. The books incorporate documentary and oral history, folklore, and informal literature in a way that makes these resources accessible to all Missourians.

Intended primarily for adult new readers, these books will also be invaluable to readers of all ages interested in the cultural and social history of Missouri.

Books in the Series

Food in Missouri: A Cultural Stew,
  by Madeline Matson

German Settlement in Missouri: New Land, Old Ways,
  by Robyn K. Burnett and Ken Luebbering

Jesse James and the Civil War in Missouri,
  by Robert L. Dyer

On Shaky Ground: The New Madrid Earthquakes of 1811–1812,
  by Norma Hayes Bagnall

Orphan Trains to Missouri,
  by Michael D. Patrick and Evelyn Goodrich Trickel

The Osage in Missouri,
  by Kristie C. Wolferman

Paris, Tightwad, and Peculiar: Missouri Place Names,
  by Margot Ford McMillen

The Trail of Tears across Missouri,
  by Joan Gilbert

Blind Boone

Missouri's Ragtime Pioneer

Jack A. Batterson

University of Missouri Press
Columbia and London

Copyright ©1998 by
The Curators of the University of Missouri
University of Missouri Press, Columbia, Missouri 65201
Printed and bound in the United States of America
All rights reserved
5 4 3 2 1 02 01 00 99 98

Library of Congress Cataloging-in-Publication Data

Batterson, Jack A., 1959–
    Blind Boone : Missouri's ragtime pioneer / Jack A. Batterson.
        p.   cm.
    Includes bibliographical references and index.
    ISBN 0-8262-1198-4 (pbk. : alk. paper)
    1. Boone, Blind, 1864–1927.   2. Composers—United States.
    3. Musicians—Missouri.   4. Ragtime music—History and
    criticism.   I. Title.
    ML410.B715B38   1998
    781.64'5'092—dc21
    [B]   98-34157
                                                                      CIP
                                                                      MN

⊚ ™   This paper meets the requirements of the
American National Standard for Permanence of Paper
for Printed Library Materials, Z39.48, 1984.

Typesetter: Crane Composition
Printer and binder: Thomson-Shore, Inc.
Typefaces: Palatino and Cheltenham
Designer: Stephanie Foley

This book has been published with the generous assistance of a gift
from the Stafford Family Charitable Trust of Columbia, Missouri.

*In memory of my father, who
taught me to appreciate history*

Contents

Acknowledgments

This study of John William "Blind" Boone brings together information from hundreds of articles and other scattered sources to provide a comprehensive picture of Boone's life and accomplishments. Misspellings and misprints in quotations from newspapers have been silently corrected throughout the book.

Much of the material has come from the Joint Collections of the State Historical Society of Missouri and the University of Missouri Western Historical Manuscript Collection in Columbia, which provided articles, documents, correspondence, photographs, and reminiscences. Other Columbia, Missouri, sources include the Boone County Historical Society, local government and newspaper files, and personal interviews.

Public and private libraries that provided helpful assistance include Ellis Library, University of Missouri–Columbia; Miller Nichols Library, University of Missouri–Kansas City; University City, Joplin, and Kansas City Public Libraries; Trails Regional Library in Warrensburg, Missouri; State Fair Community College Learning Resources Center in Sedalia, Missouri; the Washington University Music Library in St. Louis; the Black Archives of

Mid-America, Inc., in Kansas City; the Mobile, Alabama, Public Library, and The New York City Public Library.

Historical and ragtime societies have also been of great help. These include the Missouri Historical Society in St. Louis; the State Historical Society of Nebraska; the Iowa State Historical Society; the Johnson County Historical Society in Warrensburg, Missouri; the Hoosier Ragtime Society in Indianapolis; the Maple Leaf Club of Los Angeles; and the Northern Virginia Ragtime Society.

Two individuals stand out in their contributions to my work. Dr. William Parrish, Professor Emeritus of History at Mississippi State University, shared his insights and his notes on Boone material in the E. Azalia Hackley Collection in the Detroit Public Library. Also, Professor Trebor Jay Tichenor, ragtime historian at Washington University in St. Louis, shared his collection of materials and his knowledge. Both scholars were generous with their advice and suggestions. Many other scholars, librarians, ragtime enthusiasts, and acquaintances of Boone gave varied assistance to help complete this study.

A special thank you goes to Becky Schroeder, whose hours of editing and whose invaluable suggestions made the finished product possible.

Blind Boone

Chapter 1

Blind Boone and His Times

Born in poverty during the chaos of the Civil War and blind from infancy, John William "Blind" Boone managed to supplement a natural musical talent with formal training to become a well-respected concert pianist and composer. He toured widely in the United States and Canada from his home in Columbia, Missouri, leaving his mark not only through his performances on the concert stage but as an ambassador of goodwill in an era still marked by wide racial divisions.

Boone's significance as a performer and composer lies in three facets of his career. First, he combined his love for black folk music with his love for American and European classical music, performing both repertories within the same concert. By inspiring an appreciation of both styles in his audiences, many made up of rural and small-town Midwesterners, he was able to bridge the gap between popular and classical music. Secondly, Boone, a mulatto, moved comfortably, personally as well as professionally, in both black and white worlds. By bringing music of the African American tradition to white audiences and music of the European tradition to black audiences, he bridged the gap between the two races and promoted mutual appreciation of the music of both races. Finally, as a performer and a composer, Boone's own evolution from plantation melodies and the popular "coon songs" to ragtime reflects the musical trends of his day. The term *coon songs* refers to those works, especially popular in the 1890s, depicting blacks in supposedly humorous but also outrageously disparaging ways.

Boone not only pioneered in the creation of ragtime as a new musical form but also in the use of ragtime on the concert stage, bringing it legitimacy and appreciation. He became important as a composer, performer, and popularizer of ragtime as a new genre.

John William Boone's life span, 1864–1927, coincided with exciting developments in American music, both in the achievements of classical music and in the expansion of popular music in the African tradition. Eileen Southern thoroughly examined these developments in her outstanding study, *The Music of Black Americans: A History.* Southern, Professor Emerita of Music and Afro-American Studies at Harvard, is an authority on the evolution of black music in America, and this chapter makes use of her work. Tilford Brooks's *America's Black Musical Heritage* also gives detailed overviews of African American music in the United States during this period.

Musical developments at the classical level, almost wholly dominated by whites, included the rise of symphony orchestras, opera, music conservatories, and an American school of composers. African Americans in the classical field, including opera, orchestras, and the concert stage, faced such limited opportunities to perform in the United States that they generally resorted to studying and performing abroad. At the level of popular music, however, black performance ushered in an entirely new era. African Americans found opportunities in musical extravaganzas, singing groups, traveling shows, minstrelsy, brass bands, and society dance orchestras. Some became itinerant musicians, traveling from town to town to perform.

Minstrel shows were popular in the United States throughout the nineteenth century and into the early twentieth century. Minstrelsy helped popularize the banjo, which arrived in the Americas with Africans. (Courtesy of Trebor Jay Tichenor)

In composing, as in performing, blacks established a place in American culture for the African tradition in music. In the evolution of both the blues and of ragtime, blacks dominated a new culture that whites later adopted enthusiastically. This popular culture overcame racial differences and produced, with the introduction of ragtime, a truly American contribution to popular music.

Black Performers in Opera

The field of opera provided limited opportunities for blacks in the late nineteenth century, but there were two major black opera companies: the Original Colored America Opera Troupe of Washington, D.C., active in the 1870s; and the Theodore Drury Colored Opera Company, which opened in New York in 1889. Drury, one of several blacks who studied at the National Conservatory of Music in New York in the 1890s, employed some white orchestra members and some white soloists, but most of the leading roles

featured such black singers as Desseria Plato, Estelle Pick-
ney Clough, George Ruffin, and Drury himself. This company produced operas by such composers as Bizet,
Gounod, Verdi, and others.

Only Scott Joplin, of Sedalia, Missouri, became a significant black composer of opera in this early period. Joplin,
who had probably never seen or heard grand opera, wrote
two complete operas, neither successful in his lifetime. He
staged his first opera, *A Guest of Honor,* only once. Unable
to find funding for *Treemonisha,* his second opera, Joplin
performed it at Harlem Hall in 1915 without scenery, light-
ing, or costumes. The work had all the elements of a grand
opera with the use of an overture, prelude, recitatives (de-
clamatory singing in musical tones), arias, small ensem-
bles, choruses, and ballet. Joplin used folk dances and folk
songs in operatic disguise, some elements of black musical
theater, and spiritual singing to carry out his message that
education could be the salvation of the black people of the
United States. *Treemonisha* enjoyed a surge of popularity in
the 1970s, more than half a century after Joplin's death. According to Scott Joplin's biographer, Ed Berlin, it was largely
because of this opera that "the Pulitzer Committee early in
1976 awarded Joplin a special Bicentennial Pulitzer Prize
for his contributions to American music." Joplin is even
more important in musical history, however, as the major
creator of classical ragtime, which combines folk music
with the European tradition.

Classical Music

Few black orchestras existed in the United States in the
late nineteenth and early twentieth centuries. New Orleans
had two black symphony orchestras, the Lyre Club Symphony Orchestra, organized in 1897, and a community
orchestra formed by William Nickerson in the 1890s. Nickerson's orchestra played at the Great Congress in Atlanta

in 1900 and appeared in Chicago the same year. Nathaniel Clark Smith directed a short-lived orchestra in Chicago from 1902 to 1905. Edward Gilbert Anderson founded the first black orchestra in Philadelphia in 1904 and served as conductor until 1917.

A few more opportunities existed for blacks in the white-dominated field of the concert stage as singers, pianists, and violinists. Among the more famous prima donnas were Desseria Plato, who was also a New York opera star, and Annie Pindell, the "Black Nightingale," who toured in the western states. Emma Azalia Hackley studied in Detroit, graduated from the University of Denver, and became a successful concert singer and music festival organizer. Another concert star, Anita Patti Brown, toured the United States, Europe, the West Indies, and South America. Matilda Sissieretta Jones, another prima donna, studied at the Providence Academy of Music and the New England Conservatory and sang at the White House for President Benjamin Harrison in 1892. Concert star Harry T. Burleigh, the most important of the black male performers on the concert stage, sang for President Theodore Roosevelt and for King Edward VII in London. The careers of these singers lasted anywhere from three to twelve years. Concert stars who found it difficult to make a living through performing often taught music or become choir directors.

Black concert pianists, mostly men, studied in Europe as well as in the United States. Edmond Dede studied in New Orleans and Paris, centering his concert performances in New Orleans. Raymond Lawson, the first black pianist to perform concerts with a symphony orchestra, studied at the Hartford School of Music and in Europe. Nathaniel Dett, who studied at Oberlin, toured widely. Carl Diton studied in Germany as well as in the United States. In 1909, he became the first black pianist to make a transcontinental tour of the United States. Hazel Harrison, the major black female pianist, studied both in Germany and in the United States.

Black violinists, largely foreign-trained, excelled. Serving as role models for other black violinists, George Polgreen Bridgetower and Jose White achieved great fame on the concert stage. Bridgetower, who died in 1860, studied with Haydn and Beethoven, and Beethoven wrote the *Kreutzer* Sonata for him. Jose White, a Cuban, attended the Paris Conservatory and impressed American audiences in an 1876 tour of the United States. Another concert star, Joseph Douglass, became the first violinist to record his works for the Victor Talking Machine Company. Unfortunately, the recordings were never released. Clarence Cameron White, who studied in England, began playing concerts at the age of fifteen and became a concert favorite. John Thomas Douglass, solo violinist, toured with the Hyers Sisters and the Georgia Minstrels. Finally, the "Prince of Negro Violinists," Walter Craig, made his debut in 1870 in Cooper Hall in New York.

Popular Music

In contrast to the limited numbers of black performers in classical music, black participation in several forms of popular music dominated, making significant contributions to the important field of popular culture. Gigantic musical extravaganzas serve as one example of black participation in the popular culture of the 1870s and 1880s. Early extravaganzas of this type included the P. S. Gilmore's World Peace Jubilee in 1872 and the Centennial Celebration of American Independence at Philadelphia in 1876. One exhibit at the Centennial Celebration featured a plantation scene with blacks singing folk songs.

Later extravaganzas included the World's Columbian Exposition of 1893 celebrating the four hundredth anniversary (in 1892) of Columbus's discovery of America. In 1895 Billy McClain's *Black America* show played in Brooklyn and in Boston. The McClain show featured a cast of five hundred blacks in a three-part show. The first part recreated African episodes through dance and song, while the second part included American songs and dances in the European and Afro-American tradition. A cakewalk, a high-stepping march satirizing fancy-dressed whites, acted as an exciting finale. McClain's show won public acclaim and gave a clear demonstration of black musical talent.

Singing Groups

Black singing groups performing spirituals provided another source of popular entertainment. The Fisk Jubilee Singers of Fisk University in Nashville, Tennessee, pioneered in this field, meeting with great success in fundraising for the university. In seven years the Fisk Singers raised $150,000 toward the construction of Jubilee Hall. Public demand for the group led to their singing at the World Peace Jubilee in Boston in 1872. They toured throughout the United States, the British Isles, and Europe. The achievements of the Fisk Jubilee Singers led to the creation of similar university singing groups, most of which met with some success.

With the rise of black singing groups, permanently based black choral societies developed in major cities. In 1892 Henry Lewis organized one of the earliest such groups, the Amphion Glee Club of Washington, D.C. Also in Washington, John Turner Layton directed the Coleridge Taylor Choral Society after 1902. Chicago had at least several choral groups: Pedro Tinsley founded the Choral Study Club in 1900; Edward Morris and Arthur Brown organized the Umbrian Glee Club in 1908 (which remained active into the 1980s); and in 1910, James Mundy formed the Federal Glee Club, consisting of the city's black postal clerks and mail carriers. In the 1920s Mundy directed the South Side Opera Company; also, J. Wesley Jones directed the chorus of the annual Chicagoland Music Festivals for thirty years.

J. B. T. Marsh's *The Story of the Jubilee Singers*, published in Boston
in 1880, memorializes the story of the famous Fisk Jubilee Singers.
(Black Archives of Mid-America, Inc., Kansas City)

In Kansas City, Missouri, Gerald Tyler directed his Tyler
Choral Society in the early twentieth century. He later
moved to St. Louis, where he conducted community choirs
from 1911 to 1922.

Other major singing groups toured at home and abroad.
The sixteen-member Williams Jubilee Singers performed in
most of the concert halls of the United States and made several world tours from about 1915 to 1925. They sang popular ballads, plantation songs, and operatic and oratorio airs.
The most important of the numerous singing groups included the Wilmington (North Carolina) Jubilee Singers,
Slayton's Jubilee Singers, the Shepperd Jubilee Singers, and
the MacMillen and Sourbeck Jubilee Singers, later called
Stinson's Jubilee Singers.

Barbershop groups also flourished as singing groups
in this era. Blacks frequently owned the barbershops and
allowed barber-musicians to hold rehearsals in the back

room when they had no patrons. From this tradition, black male groups proliferated rapidly, no longer limiting themselves to barbers as members. Barbershop groups gave rise to such famous singers as Richard Milburn, Sam Lucas, and Buddy Bolden and provided opportunities for male singers. Men had met with much less success than black women in finding a place on the concert stage. Successful male groups included Lew's Male Quartet of New England, managed by William Lew; Lew's Male Quintette, managed by M. Hamilton Hodges; and the Golden Gate Quartet of Baltimore.

Religious Music

Black singing groups relied heavily on religious music in their performances. Tilford Brooks describes three types of religious music that served as the core of their repertoire. First, the *spiritual,* with its lyrical quality, allowed a wide range of emotions, such as elation, hope, or sorrow; this type of singing reflected the holy spirit most closely. The second type, the *jubilee,* came from the heart of an individual as an exultant song but did not closely reflect the Holy Spirit. The *shout,* the last type, refers to either of the first two types performed in dance form.

The African musical tradition provided the inspiration for the black spiritual, rooted either in melodies indigenous to Africa or melodies created in America from the African tradition. Spirituals grew rapidly in popularity after emancipation because of the great expansion of black churches. According to Eileen Southern, these churches continued the African tradition in a variety of ways through spirit possessions, holy dancing, speaking in tongues, improvisational singing, use of drums, shouting, hand clapping, jubilee songs, and ecstatic seizures.

Arrangers and publishers soon came forth to meet the popular demand for this type of music. For example, Harry

Thacker Burleigh became a popular arranger, while Marshall W. Taylor published the first hymnal after emancipation, *A Collection of Revival Hymns and Plantation Melodies* (1883).

Traveling Shows

The growth of such traveling shows as the Uncle Tom's Cabin Company provided another form of popular entertainment in the late nineteenth century. Traveling shows also provided new opportunities for blacks, many of whom began their careers as a "pickaninny" or a singer in plantation scenes in such a company. The shows often opened with scenes showing the hardships blacks had suffered in slavery. Charles Turner organized a typical traveling show, *In Old Kentucky*, first staged in 1892. The show featured a twenty-four-piece band, the Whangdoodles. Another 1890s traveling show, *The South before the War*, made heavy use of plantation scenes, camp meetings, and cakewalks. A similar company, the Hyers Sisters Musical Comedy Company, which evolved into a comic opera company in 1876, used an all-black repertoire as early as the 1870s. It persisted into the 1890s.

Blacks also found performing opportunities with the Sells Brothers and Forepaugh's Circus, which employed Billy McClain as their first black member in 1886. Many black groups had a national following, and their itineraries were reported in such black newspapers as the *Indianapolis Freeman*, the *Cleveland Gazette*, the *New York Globe*, and the *New York Age*.

Minstrels

Minstrelsy, originally called "the Ethiopian business," achieved great popular success in the 1870s and 1880s. It re-

(Courtesy of Trebor Jay
Tichenor)

flected, in its early forms, white exploitation of blacks,
deriding the "Ethiopian" origins of black music. Minstrels
first featured caricatures of blacks performed by whites in
blackface. Later, blacks themselves performed minstrel
songs and skits. The Georgia Minstrels, organized in 1865 by
George B. Hicks, became the first successful all-black minstrel company. This group used several names, according to
Tilford Brooks: Callender's Georgia Minstrels, Haverly's
European Minstrels, and finally Callender's Consolidated
Minstrels. The group was not typical in that it combined
serious music with minstrel music, but its fame spread in the
1870s and 1880s. Other minstrel groups of the era included
Sprague's Georgia Minstrels, W. S. Cleveland's Big Colored
Minstrels, Lew Dockstader's Minstrels, Richard's and
Pringle's Minstrels, and Al G. Field's Negro Minstrels.

The typical small minstrel company led a marginal exis-
tence. Such companies, usually including only two or three
musicians, often had to make their own scenery and provide their own footlights as well as clean the hall after each

performance. As blacks, they had difficulty in finding lodging and frequently had to sleep in the concert halls or in train stations. Life for performers in larger minstrel companies was somewhat easier, but only the most successful members could travel in Pullman cars, which served as sleeping quarters. An indication of the prejudice they suffered is seen in Eileen Southern's description of signs in southern towns warning: "Nigger, Don't Let the Sun Go Down On You!" or "Nigger, Read and Run."

While the small minstrel companies advertised by playing in factories during lunch hours, the large groups marched through town with impressive bands, performing classical overtures and popular songs to attract attention. Minstrel companies recruited and trained their own apprentices, first accepting only black men but later adding black women to the companies. Eileen Southern has described the program of a typical large minstrel show. It might last almost two hours and usually included three parts. The first part of the show featured a band elevated on a stage. Next came an *olio,* a variety show of specialty acts. The finale included the entire company.

The minstrel band played a central role in the success of the show. Musicians were versatile and hardworking; they usually were expected to play more than one instrument. Most marched in the parade; for example the W. A. Mahara Minstrels had a thirty-three-piece band for their parade and forty-two musicians in the show. Bandleaders wore brightly colored uniforms, which usually included a silk hat. Their duties included training and rehearsing the band, coaching the soloists, making orchestrations, and even composing music. Music for parades included marches by W. P. Chambers, C. W. Dalbey, and C. L. Barnhouse; "Dixie" and tunes by Stephen Foster were also popular. Music for the evening show consisted of new music composed for the minstrel company or unusual arrangements of popular pieces; some singers wrote their own songs. Typical minstrel songs included ballads, comic songs, and specialties as the three main categories.

Several minstrel performers and composers became well known in the early twentieth century. James Bland, William Kersands, and Samuel Lucas enjoyed special renown. Bland, who began his minstrel career in 1875, had attended Howard University. He became famous both as a composer and as a singer, composing some seven hundred songs, including his own version of "Carry Me Back to Old Virginny." He worked with the Black Diamond Troupe of Boston, the Bohee Brothers, Sprague's Georgia Minstrels, Haverly's Genuine Colored Minstrels, and Black Patti's Troubadours. Samuel Lucas, another minstrel star, published his works in the *Sam Lucas Plantation Songster* (ca. 1875), the *Sam Lucas Careful Man Songster* (1881), and *The Folio*. He performed in the 1870s with Lew Johnson Plantation Minstrels and with the Hyers Sisters Comic Opera Company. In 1878, he became the first African American to play the title role in *Uncle Tom's Cabin*. Minstrel star William (Billy) Kersands toured with Barney Hicks Georgia Minstrels and with the Hyers Sisters.

Black Theaters

The success of black popular entertainment led to the establishment of black theaters. Chicago's Pekin Theatre, founded by Robert Mott in 1905, became the first black-owned theater in the United States and brought black entertainers before the public in musicals and other productions. Other theaters established by blacks included the Lincoln and the Lafayette in New York; the New Standard and the Dunbar, both owned by John Gibson in Philadelphia; the Booker T. Washington, owned by Charles Turpin in St. Louis; and the Howard in Washington, D.C.

Bands

Bands, especially brass bands, provided another form of entertainment and employment for blacks. U.S. Army bands, society dance orchestras, and itinerant musical groups added to the variety of bands used for minstrels and road shows. Some superior army brass bands toured small frontier towns. One U.S. Army band consisting of black musicians, the Ninth Cavalry Band, played in Billy McClain's *Black America* in 1895. New Orleans, as a major center of black culture, had the largest number of brass bands, including the Excelsior, Kelly's, the Onward, and the St. Bernard brass bands.

Some black musicians played in white brass bands. For example, Henderson Smith reportedly played in Patrick Gilmore's Famous Cornet Band. Eileen Southern states that other blacks sometimes "passed" for white in order to have opportunities to perform more.

Society dance orchestras also rose in demand, playing in dance halls, in stage concerts, and with choral groups. Musicians often doubled by playing in brass bands and also playing a string or wind instrument in a dance orchestra. One famous society dance orchestra, the Craig Celebrated Orchestra, organized in 1872, offered black musicians a start in their professional careers. Alfred Mando showed his versatility by performing with his New York dance orchestra as well as with the Mozart Conservatory Concert Orchestra.

Itinerant or community musicians performed in bands or as individuals. Small groups sometimes wandered from town to town, but most itinerants traveled and played alone. Such musicians had little if any formal training and could not get jobs in professional groups. They usually had no fixed itinerary but gave recitals on street corners and in restaurants, passing a hat to collect money before moving on to the next town. Those who did not travel often played organ or piano music in churches, opera houses, dance halls, or saloons. Others followed a seasonal route and sang on trains or provided entertainment as waiters for patrons on riverboats on the Ohio, Missouri, and Mississippi Rivers.

The Development of Ragtime

Although blacks were active in the many forms of popular culture, they perhaps made their most significant contribution in the creation of new musical forms, including ragtime, which derived almost entirely from the African American tradition.

The ragtime era, 1896–1913, is a musical reflection of many of the social changes of the time. The period after Reconstruction ended in 1877 saw the return of control to white leadership in the South, making life especially difficult for blacks. According to the historian John Hope Franklin in *From Slavery to Freedom,* secret societies such as the Knights of the White Camelia and the Knights of the Ku Klux Klan engaged in "intimidation, force, ostracism in business and society, bribery at the polls, arson, and even murder to accomplish their deals." Over twenty-five hundred lynchings in the last sixteen years of the nineteenth century, and eleven hundred from the turn of the century to World War I, emphasized the insecurity of blacks throughout the country. After segregation was legalized on railroads by *Plessy v. Ferguson* in 1896, the passing of Jim Crow laws forcing segregation in society became a common practice in many state legislatures. President Woodrow Wilson even segregated federal employees by executive order, and many Indiana towns prohibited black residents within the city limits. Problems were compounded by black population shifts, and as the migration of blacks to the North grew, hostility in northern states increased.

Eileen Southern identifies the ragtime years as a transition era in black music, reflecting the new mobility and freedom to travel. The black populations of New York and Philadelphia grew to about 50,000 each by 1900. Chicago's black population increased from 4,000 to nearly 15,000 in the late 1800s. In the decade after 1910, roughly 330,000 southern blacks moved to northern and western states. These included black musicians who brought their own style north, resulting in the "Chicago syncopated style" and similar movements in cities like Detroit and Denver. This distinctive style reflected the new national African American school of music, which defied old forms and showed particular enthusiasm for folk music.

In the early twentieth century, blacks faced conditions more challenging than at any time since the Civil War. Their position in American society is reflected in the slanderous lyrics of coon songs. As the music historian John Hasse notes, it is "one of the great ironies of the Ragtime Era that the lyrics of racially demeaning songs were frequently set to ragtime—a music created by the very people denigrated by the songs." However, ragtime served as a positive influence in this difficult period. It not only provided an outlet for black expression, but its popularity with whites became a source of interracial appreciation.

The origin of rag songs, according to the music historian and ragtime performer Terry Waldo, is as old as slavery in America. It comes partly from the application by slaves of African rhythmic styles to European music and partly from the later heritage of black spirituals, camp meetings, plantation dances, slave work songs, minstrel shows, and marching songs. Coon songs and cakewalks were natural sources of ragtime music. Ragtime itself may be the result of conventionally trained musicians who also used black folk sources.

Musicologists continue to argue about the source of the term "ragtime," but all agree on its African American roots and its importance as a truly American contribution to popular music. The words *ragged* or *broken time* were used for New Orleans dance music as early as 1886. The application of these words came with Ernest Hogan's "All Coons Look Alike" and Ben Harney's "You've Been a Good Old Wagon but You've Don Broke Down," both in 1896. The term *ragtime* applies especially to the peculiar broken rhythmic features of coon songs. To "rag" is to syncopate the melody of nonsyncopated work. Many rags were actually improvisations of existing popular songs and were never written down. Some surprising examples of ragging of written music noted by Hasse include the "Russian Rag," based on Rachmaninoff's Prelude in C-sharp Minor; a Liszt-based "Hungarian Rag"; and rags based on Mendelssohn's "Spring Song" and "Wedding March"; Rubenstein's "Melody in F"; and John Philip Sousa's "Stars and Stripes Forever."

The spread of ragtime brought public exposure of this new musical form and more job opportunities for black musicians. The public heard ragtime in the World's Columbian Exposition of 1893 in Chicago, the Trans-Mississippi Exposition at Omaha in 1899, the Pan-American Fair at Buffalo in 1901, and the St. Louis Exposition of 1904. It appeared as early as 1888 in the slums of St. Louis and flourished especially in New Orleans, St. Louis, and Chicago. Vaudeville, well established by the ragtime era, and piano playing in movie houses also expanded job opportunities. The coming of the phonograph and the gramophone increased access to popular music, and those who could afford them also used player pianos and piano rolls.

Ragtime was associated with the piano from the beginning, and the piano was the sole instrument used in the saloons and brothel houses where ragtime was born. The rise of the piano's popularity corresponded with the flourishing of ragtime itself. The ability of the middle class to afford popular entertainment and musical education further increased the demand for the piano. According to Hasse, sales of the instrument reached a peak in 1909; the popularity of player-piano ragtime reflects the excitement generated by the flashy effects of playing that had been edited to add extra notes, enhance the volume, and eliminate mistakes.

Piano rags were of several varieties. They could be piano arrangements of a coon song, the ragging of nonsyncopated works, original compositions, or ragged versions of European classics. The words *rag* and *dance* were used interchangeably. Blind Boone's "When I Meet Dat Coon To-night" was called a dance but was in fact a rag that he wrote as early as 1892. Boone has been neglected as a pioneer in classical ragtime, although his music shows some of the characteristics used in classical rags. He never limited himself to rags, and his neglect by historians may stem partly from his use of so many musical forms in his concerts and compositions and the fact that he did not concentrate solely on ragtime; his emphasis throughout his career on concert touring rather than composing may also account for the failure to recognize his contributions to the form.

There is certainly agreement that Scott Joplin, "The King of Ragtime," remains the most important ragtime composer. Joplin created classical ragtime by applying rag syncopation to European music. After spending a decade in St. Louis, he made Sedalia, Missouri, a ragtime center. His "Maple Leaf Rag," published in 1899 and named after the Maple Leaf Cafe, where he played, was a huge success and became a model for other ragtime composers. Scott Hayden and Arthur Marshall, students of Joplin, were also important as composers and performers. James Scott of Carthage, Missouri, probably ranks next to Joplin in importance. Scott organized an orchestra in Kansas City and composed as well. Also of major importance are Joseph Lamb, a white New York ragtime composer, and Tom

Turpin. According to Eileen Southern, Turpin's "Harlem Rag" (1897) was the first published piano rag composed by a black man. Kansas City produced the composer Arthur Pryor, who also played trombone with Sousa's band. Ben Harney in New Orleans set the stage for such later ragtime composers as Jelly Roll Morton and Tony Jackson. There were several hundred publishers of ragtime, but John Stark of Sedalia, who later established his company in St. Louis, stands out as a popularizer of ragtime with his publication of such composers as Scott Joplin, James Scott, Joseph Lamb, Arthur Marshall, and Artie Matthews.

Ragtime influenced American society in several ways. As Southern and Tilford both note, its most profound impact may be through its evolution into the blues and jazz in the early twentieth century. Certainly the blues originates from such black experiences as were voiced in black spirituals, the themes of loneliness and hardship and expressions of despair and sorrow, all traits common in black music. Performers illustrated these traits through such singing styles as blue notes, falsetto, moaning, and groaning. By the 1920s, the blues had led to the rise of such singers as Son House, Robert Johnson, Blind Lemon Jefferson, Lightin' Hopkins, Brownie McGhee, and Sonny Terry. Female singers included Bessie Smith, Ma Rainey, Bertha Hill, Hociel Thomas, Ida Cox, and Sippie Wallace. William Christopher Handy, one of the most famous black composers and publishers of blues, became famous for his "Memphis Blues" and "St. Louis Blues."

Ragtime, by combining African and European antecedents, evolved into one of the first truly American contributions to music. It brought black musical traits and rhythms into acceptance by white Americans, leading to a flourishing new popular culture. For example, piano rag music, according to Eileen Southern, featured foot stomping and patting the keys with the left hand while the right hand played syncopated tunes reminiscent of fiddle and banjo tunes. Along with this came a whole new body of musical literature and a musical form that continues to engender enthusiasm with its successive revivals.

Black music of African heritage had come into its own in Blind Boone's era, with performers and composers in the United States and abroad. The use of such African instruments as the banjo and spirited performing styles affected work songs, spirituals, ragtime, blues, and, eventually, jazz, all of which derived from these origins. Even the white-dominated concert stage music borrowed some African traits. Although whites largely controlled European classical "serious" music, black composers and performers provided much of the popular music, all of which greatly enriched the American musical traditions of the era.

Blind Boone's career, encompassing the whole of the ragtime era, demonstrated the very evolution of the musical forms of the era itself. His own troubled beginnings and overcoming of hardships are also symbolic of the times.

Chapter 2

A Troubled Beginning

The lack of complete information concerning Boone's birth and parentage reflects the chaotic conditions of blacks in Missouri toward the end of the Civil War. Information in Melissa Fuell's *Blind Boone: His Early Life and His Achievements* is based on interviews with Boone when she sang with the Blind Boone Concert Company. Although several sources give Boone's birth date as March 1864, Fuell's date of May 17, 1864, is commonly used. In spite of later claims that he was born in Warrensburg, Fuell confirmed that his birth actually took place in Miami, Missouri, in a Union army camp occupied by the Seventh Militia, Company I.

According to Fuell, a Civil War veteran named Charles Smith contacted Boone in De Soto, Iowa, in the winter of 1915 when Boone was on tour there. Smith later remarked, "I was in camp the morning that man was born, I remember his mother, Rachel, very well indeed. She cooked for our regiment. Many of us that morning in May went to her quarters to see the new baby." Boone reportedly choked with sobs at the reference to his beloved mother.

Questions also remain regarding Rachel Boone, his mother. Born a slave, she belonged to the descendants of Daniel Boone. Toward the end of the Civil War, she gained

Boone's mother, Rachel Boone, took her name from the family who once owned her, relatives of Daniel Boone. (State Historical Society of Missouri, Columbia)

her freedom by fleeing to Union lines, where she became a cook for the Union army. Some sources stated that Rachel Boone was related to Daniel Boone, but in fact her name resulted from the common practice of slaves adopting the surnames of their owners.

In the absence of any lasting relationship between his parents, Boone grew up with his mother's name, and no record remains of any clear identity of his father. There is disagreement about whether the father was a white drum major, as an article in the *Warrensburg Star Journal* in 1927 claimed, or a bugler, as other sources report. Judge George Moore, who had known Boone, recalled in 1951 that Boone was "coffee-colored" and assumed that both parents were black. However, in an interview in 1951, William R. Gentry of Columbia asserted that Boone was a mulatto, born of a black mother and a white father. Boone's appearance would seem to verify this.

Shortly after Boone's birth, his mother moved with him to Warrensburg, Missouri. A growing city of about eight thousand during Boone's youth, Warrensburg became important as the county seat of Johnson County. The town

A simple drawing of Boone's childhood home in Warrensburg was published in *Blind Boone: His Early Life and Achievements,* by Melissa Fuell, in 1915. (State Historical Society of Missouri, Columbia)

claimed several famous citizens, including Governor Thomas T. Crittenden, General and Senator Francis M. Cockrell, mathematician Reuben Fields, and Columbia Morrow, who had been chief clerk of the U.S. Senate. Warrensburg proved to be a congenial setting for the development of Boone's talents.

When Boone was about six months old, he contracted what doctors then called "brain fever," an illness accompanied by a high fever. Again, sources disagree. George Ashley blamed a common cold for his condition in *Reminiscences of a Circuit Rider,* published in 1941. The historian William Parrish suggests, in a *Missouri Life* article of November 1979, that Boone more likely suffered from encephalitis or meningitis. What is known is that Boone fell victim to the contemporary medical practice of removing the patient's eyes surgically to relieve the pressure on the brain. His eyelids were then sewn shut. Even this tragic episode in Boone's life seems shrouded in mystery. Reports disagree not only on the nature of Boone's illness but also concerning his age when he lost his sight. Nonetheless, the removal of his eyes was believed to have saved Boone's life. Dr. Loren Humphrey, a retired professor of surgery in Columbia, believes that Boone had *Ophthalmia neonatorum,* a frequent cause of blindness in newborns before the use of silver nitrate drops. Dr. Humphrey concludes that the condition must have been severe enough to lead to the medical decision to remove his eyes, which were probably scarred and blind; the removal, as with many amputations in those days, was undoubtedly performed to prevent death from systemic spread of the infection.

Remarkably, Boone's happiness as a child and as an adult was seemingly not hampered by the loss of his sight. He felt that his other senses compensated for his blindness, becoming "proportionately sharpened." Boone's explanation was reprinted in a *Warrensburg Star Journal* article of March 20, 1981:

> Blindness has not affected my disposition. It has never made me at outs with the world. . . . I have shown that no matter how a person is afflicted, there is something that he can do worth while. . . . I regard my blindness as a blessing for had I not been blind I would not have given the inspiration to the world that I have.

Rachel Boone worked as a domestic servant in the homes of several prosperous families in Warrensburg. Her employment in white households introduced "Little Willie" into the white world, in which he became quite comfortable. Color was apparently not an important factor to him or to the white families. He not only played with the white children of his mother's employers but also appeared to be readily accepted by both the children and their parents as an easy-going, likable child. Melissa Fuell described "Willie" as a poor but happy and healthy boy, full of pranks,

Senator Francis Marion Cockrell and his family on the front porch steps of his home in Warrensburg, Missouri. Boone's mother, Rachel, worked for several families in Warrensburg, including the Cockrell family. (State Historical Society of Missouri, Columbia)

with a cheerful disposition and a joke and a smile for everyone. In fact, he became a favorite of the community.

Many years later, Mrs. Sam Davis described Boone's childhood days in a letter reprinted in the *Warrensburg Star Journal* 1981 article. As a girl, she had lived near the home where Rachel Boone worked. Her remembrance gives the first hint of Boone's musical interests:

> He was then a small child, playing around his mother's skirts or tagging after the white children, chattering an imitation of them, calling their attention to the whistle or song of a bird, asking many questions, or quietly slipping through the sitting room into the parlor when someone would be playing the old square piano. . . . He knew the

voices and could detect the footsteps of everyone with whom he came in contact. This was true not only of children, but also of older persons. . . . Often, when he was very young his playmates would try to "slip up" on him, but always unsuccessfully. Although sightless, he was never deceived as to their identity. "Oh, I know you," he would exclaim, identifying the stealthy one by his right name. . . .

His talent for music was noticeable at an early age. His imitation of birds and other sounds of nature made him happy and never failed to amuse the crowd in which he moved. When he was still a boy someone in Warrensburg gave him a large harmonica or mouth organ. In a short time he was mouthing it with considerable skill and many an audience collected around the big tree near his home, or downtown on the streets, to hear him play and watch him as, weaving back and forth, he kept the time. And listening to that music from an instrument that in these days has sunk to a low estate, we marvelled at its sweetness, at that quality it seemed to have of being the vehicle of our deepest inner thoughts. . . .

Quite early in life the piano seemed to attract him. Whenever one of us children happened to be practicing our music lesson, he would usually be wandering near as though fascinated.

As we were not blessed with a piano in our home, much of my practicing was done on the old square piano in the home where Aunt Rachel and Blind Boone lived [it was common practice for whites to call older black women "aunt"]. "Chopsticks" and "Silvery Waves" often rang through that home. One day my teacher assigned me a new piece of music, "Sultan Polka." The catchy strains of this composition delighted little Willie Boone and he begged for a chance to play it too. He was given the opportunity and after some perseverance and a little of my assistance, his first imitation was accomplished on the piano.

Melissa Fuell reports that by age three Boone was attracting the attention of passersby with "the rhythmic tunes he would beat on a tin pan, keeping perfect time with his little feet and swaying to and fro with his body." During a 1924 interview, reported in the *Warrensburg Star Journal* of June 22, 1927, Boone fondly remembered:

> My mother was a wash woman. I use to sit out in front of the house of an evening and beat upon a tin pan with a stick and sing: "Come Rachel Boone, Come Rachel Boone; Time you's here getting Johnnie Boone's supper." . . . one evening I was sitting out in front of the senator's house beating my pan and Mrs. Cockrell said, "here you are beating on that pan trying to make Rachel hear you. We heard you away down the street and stopped at the tin shop and bought you a new pan. This is bigger and will make more noise. Beat it just as hard as you can."

Boone received his first musical instrument, a tin whistle, at the age of five. With this instrument he repeated tunes he had heard, created original melodies, and imitated calls of birds and animals. He frequently wandered about town as he played his whistle, looking like a ragged urchin, according to Fuell. People often invited him into their homes, and he seemed quite at ease as they gave him food and visited with him.

Boone began to make money with his music early in life. According to a *Columbia Missourian* article of August 25, 1921, Boone recalled that he organized a band at the age of five:

> I organized a band of seven little boys in Warrensburg at that time. I was the youngest and the leader of the band. We had two horns, two french harps [harmonicas], a drum and a comb. I was the teacup artist. When I was about nine the boys got mad and quit because they said I kept most all we made.

A "tea cup artist" covered a mouth harp (harmonica) with a tea cup to get a distinctive sound while playing. Boone's

BOONE'S LITTLE TIN WHISTLE BAND

"Little Willie Was the Leader and Would Work For Hours With the Other Boys," etc.

Boone's early "Tin Whistle Band." This drawing is from Melissa Fuell's biography. (State Historical Society of Missouri, Columbia)

band evolved according to available talent and played at picnics and around town, with Boone passing the hat for pennies.

When Boone was eight, Rachel Boone married Harrison Hendrix, who was already the father of five children. The whole family lived in a one-room cabin. Fuell described their house, which stood just behind Old Land Fike's Mill on Mill Street in Warrensburg, as a "one-room log cabin with the old puncheon floor; very scantily furnished with the real necessities of life, as it took much of the space for Mr. Hendrix's large family." With Rachel Boone's marriage, she and her son no longer lived in the employers' homes, depriving Boone of his close association with white playmates. These early childhood ties, however, allowed him to be at ease in the white world and to be comfortable in the presence of both races for the rest of his life.

Boone's local popularity led to an opportunity that was to change the course of his life. Some leading citizens of Warrensburg determined that he should have a formal education. According to the Boone interview in the *Warrensburg Star Journal* of June 22, 1927:

> The citizens of Warrensburg thought I'd do something with my talent if I had a chance, so they told my mother that I ought to be sent to the State institution for the blind at St. Louis. I was nine years old then, and as bright as any boy could be. My mother protested that she had no money to send me to school. That was in August. In September some Warrensburg citizens come in with some clothes for me and said, "Well my boy, you're going to school Monday." I asked if there would be any music there and they said that was just what they were sending me for. "We want you to go and then come back and show Warrensburg what you can do," they told me.

Senator Cockrell asked the county court to provide Boone with railroad fare and incidental expenses, and several wealthy citizens contributed sufficient funds to enable him to attend the St. Louis School for the Blind. Boone left for St. Louis in the fall of 1873, sent on his way by a large crowd at the train station. According to John Wright's *Discovering African-American St. Louis,* the Missouri Institution for the Education of the Blind had six black students when Boone arrived.

Boone loved the music at the school, but he despised his classes. In his second term, he was placed in the school's trade department where he made brooms; he spent his spare time listening to other students practicing their music. Fortunately, Enoch Donley, a senior and the son of a

St. Louis merchant, befriended "Johnny" Boone. Donley often invited Boone to listen to his practicing and sympathized with Boone's pleas to be allowed to take piano lessons. Boone was miserable until Donley finally gave him an opportunity to play. According to Fuell, Donley became "one of his dearest friends, his first and only real teacher." She described his first lesson:

> Mr. Donley could see a little, so he led Johnny to the piano and showed him the middle of the keyboard. Then he began the usual routine of finger exercises and to learn the value of the notes, i.e., whole, half, quarter, sixteenths, etc. When he had finished that lesson Johnny began to play a few strains of a very beautiful and difficult selection he had heard so often by Mr. Donley. Mr. Donley immediately stopped him and told him that it was improper to learn that way, but if he would only be patient in time he would be taught all of those things.

Since all the practice hours were taken, Boone could practice only on an old piano stored on the upper floor of the school. When Donley bragged to his music teacher about Boone's talent, the teacher agreed to listen to him play. According to Fuell:

> When Johnny learned that he was to exhibit his talent, his whole mind was given to his music. Oh, how hard he practiced. Teachers complained to the superintendent that he was missing his classes and even when he was present, he did not know his lessons.
>
> On that day that Johnny was to play his selection, the professor stole into the room, unnoticed, just as Mr. Donley had started him to play.
>
> So perfect was the time, so expressive the interpretation that the professor exclaimed to Mr. Donley, "He's a genius." To Johnny he spoke words of encouragement and left the room full of wonder and amazement.

Boone became proficient at the piano in less than a year, and he could soon play anything that he heard. His life was much happier for the rest of that year. The superintendent of the school began to invite Boone to his home to entertain his friends. When he went home for the summer, he played the piano for church services and for socials, increasing his repertoire greatly.

School life took a drastic turn for the worse in Boone's second year, when he experienced much stronger racial prejudice with the coming of a new administration at the school. A new superintendent and new teachers made things difficult with their enforcement of new rules. Boone found such treatment hard to take, and he looked for an escape. He began sneaking out of the dormitory at night, not to return for several days. These excursions generally were to the St. Louis tenderloin district, where the black population gathered to hear ragtime. It was hardly the place for a young boy. The area took its name from a New York City precinct where police officers found luscious opportunities for graft because of illegal activities such as gambling and prostitution. A number of other cities, including St. Louis, borrowed the term for areas of similar activities. After repeated escapes lasting two or three days at a time, Boone faced possible expulsion from school.

The superintendent tried to encourage Boone to behave by offering him an opportunity to play before a panel of "distinguished visitors" coming for an evaluation of the school. Boone's benefactor, Senator Cockrell, was among the visitors. An elated Boone took advantage of the offer. He played "Charming Thoughts Schottische" and, according to Fuell, "left his audience spellbound with wonder and admiration."

Boone's reform was short-lived, however, and he returned repeatedly to his favorite places on Franklin Avenue in St. Louis. He was finally expelled after two and a half years at the school. In his 1921 interview in the

Columbia Missourian, Boone recalled that he remained at the school until he was about twelve, "But they wouldn't let me play the piano all the time—they made me make brooms—so I ran off." In the interview with the *Warrensburg Star Journal,* June 22, 1927, Boone elaborated:

> The instructors down there tried to teach me how to make brooms, chair bottoms, and how to read, but I begged for music. After I had learned the distances on the keyboard I began grabbing music. In two months I was away past what my instructor was giving me.

Boone so dreaded facing his family following his expulsion that he stayed in St. Louis playing ragtime along Franklin Avenue and Morgan Street. After several days of hunger and hardship, the twelve-year-old boy made friends with an A. J. Kerry, a conductor of the Frisco Railroad Company. Kerry gave the boy food and money, and Boone's talent won him a free ride home. Kerry convinced a conductor of the Missouri Pacific Railroad to allow Boone to ride home free in return for playing the harmonica for passengers. In spite of his fears, Boone got a warm welcome in Warrensburg and was hired the next fall by Foster School to play for the students as they marched to and from classes. However Boone still faced hard times as he struggled to find a place for himself in the entertainment field. Restless and bored, he left home in the spring with his "penny-whistle" band, consisting of a tambourine, a triangle, and a mouth harp. Traveling with his band, Boone caught the attention of a gambler, Mark Cromwell. Cromwell lured the boy on with promises of clothes, food, and money. He also promised to keep Boone's mother posted and to send her money. However, he kept none of his promises, providing little food, scant clothing, and no money. When Boone complained, Cromwell scolded and whipped him. Fuell reports that Cromwell made Boone "barnstorm central Missouri, playing local halls and frequently being forced to walk from one town to another."

During this period of turmoil and confusion, Boone actually served as an item of property during a card game in Columbia. Cromwell forfeited him to Sam Reiter, who promised to free the boy from abuse. Reiter gave Boone whistles, candies, and food but left him locked in an attic for three days and three nights. When he finally allowed Boone to play in the yard, Cromwell found him and coaxed him back by telling him that Reiter would keep him prisoner. Although Boone found that Cromwell had not changed, he decided to make the best of the situation. At times Cromwell even disguised Boone as a girl in order to escape his creditors as they traveled through central Missouri.

Fortunately, Boone's stepfather, Harrison Hendrix, pursued the pair, catching up with them at Laddonia, Missouri. He gave them permission to go on to Vandalia, but he took Boone into custody after the performance there. With the help of his stepfather, friends, and police, Boone finally returned home safely. Elated to be home and secure, Boone later relished telling stories about his adventures with Cromwell and Reiter.

Boone's restlessness soon became evident again after he returned to Warrensburg. He worked once again at Foster School for about a month before deciding to leave home to find his fortune. He again earned transportation on trains by playing his "harp" and singing, living on passengers' tips. During his travels Boone met Tom Johnson, a banjo picker from Sedalia, and Ben Franklin, who called himself the "Tea Cup Artist." According to William Parrish's *Missouri Life* article, Franklin would "put a mouth harp in a tea cup to create a novel warbling sound." The trio joined forces for a few months, traveling free on trains between Mexico and Glasgow, Missouri. They did well financially and shared their earnings equally.

Ironically, the trains later became full of performers pretending to be blind or crippled, and passengers finally began to complain. The railroads were forced to make rules forbidding free transportation to wandering musicians. Boone's group finally disbanded when he refused to share a full cup of money he had collected at Glasgow, and he entered a new phase of his career. He played in black churches at Glasgow and Fayette, where he became a friend of the Reverend Jeffries of the Methodist Episcopal Church of Glasgow. Boone and Jeffries toured together for about three months, playing concerts throughout Iowa until their travel expenses forced them to return to Glasgow. Jeffries then sent Boone to the Rev. John Lee, minister of the Methodist Episcopal Church in Fayette, where Boone played for services and taught music.

Chapter 3

Launching a Career

In 1879, the Reverend Edward Stewart, pastor of the Second Baptist Church in Columbia, arranged for Boone to play in the annual Christmas concert in Columbia. This performance led to a meeting that was to have a major effect on his life. Stewart told John Lange Jr., a black contractor and philanthropist, about Boone. Lange, who acted as an organizer of his church's annual Christmas festival, asked Stewart to bring Boone to see him. The meeting of Lange and Boone was perhaps the most significant event of Boone's career. It marked the beginning of a long and close friendship.

Lange may have heard Boone play previously and recognized upon meeting him that the young man would make the Christmas festival a success. He paid Boone well for his performance at the festival and treated him kindly. After this, Boone stayed mostly in Columbia.

He had been in Columbia several months when an already famous black blind pianist, Blind Tom, came to town in 1880. An inevitable comparison and rivalry began between the two pianists that lasted even beyond Blind Tom's death in 1908.

Blind Tom, Thomas Green Bethune, was born a slave on May 25, 1849, on Wiley Edward Jones's plantation in Harris County, Georgia. He belonged to Colonel James N.

Blind Tom had toured extensively by the time he appeared in Columbia in 1880. (Boone County Historical Society, Columbia)

Bethune, who rented him in 1858 to Perry Oliver for a three-year period. Oliver took Tom on tours, including a tour abroad in 1866. He toured Europe and South America as well as the United States as a vaudeville attraction. Blind Tom advertised that he could play seven thousand pieces upon request and that he had composed over one hundred pieces. He published his music under such pseudonyms as J. C. Beckel and Francois Setalise. He retired in 1898 but made a comeback tour in 1904–1905.

Blind Tom was said to be a "semi-idiot," and his uncontrolled body had to be strapped to a piano bench for his performances. The article in the *Columbia Missouri Herald* of February 26, 1880, to promote Tom's Columbia appearance represents the attitudes toward the musician exhibited by some:

> Whoever has failed to attend the marvelous performances of Blind Tom . . . ought not to neglect the present opportunity. Of mere music the public have an abundant supply; but when it emanates from a condition of idiocy, when you might as well expect one of the orangoutangs from Barnum's Cage to step on the stage and reproduce the most exquisite creations of the masters, as to see the thing really done by this poor demented negro; when you see his sight-

less eyes wandering in vacancy, and his tongue lapping his lips as if he were turning some sweet morsel while a flow of melody is pouring from beneath his fingers, it is impossible not to wonder at the mysterious dispensation of Providence that has bestowed upon this nonentity—this being so little higher than a brute—one of the choicest of gifts and the ability to illustrate that gift . . . , but how he does it is a problem that is not likely to be solved this side of eternity. Last evening he was in fine humor and played at his best, giving not only repetitions of such works as the "Rhapsodie Hongroise," "Trovatore," "Pleyel's Hymn," with variations, and national melodies of different countries, but introducing novel and startling effects of his own. Two or three of his original songs were full of exquisite beauty, and his composition descriptive of the Battle of Manassas lost none of its freshness or quaintness from the fact that it has been heard scores of times before. As a musical phenomenon, without other intelligence than that which is conveyed from a single organ in his brain to his fingers, Blind Tom is undoubtedly the most remarkable prodigy in Christendom.

Garth Hall (later Haden Opera House) on East Broadway provided the setting for the March 3, 1880, concert by Blind Tom, initiating the rivalry between the two blind pianists. On March 5, 1880, the *Columbia Missourian Statesman* reported on the concert: ". . . the largest crowd ever in Garth Hall, filling floor, gallery and even part of the stage, paid their way the previous night to witness the performance of Blind Tom. . . ." Much of the excitement may have stemmed from the fact that Lange intended to bring the fifteen-year-old Blind Boone to challenge Blind Tom. According to an article in the *Columbia Tribune* of July 25, 1912:

After Tom's famous "Battle of Manassas" and other star renditions, two or three musicians, among them Miss Campbell, teacher of music in Christian College, now Mrs.

Blind Boone made his first major Columbia appearance in the "play-off" with Blind Tom at age fifteen. (State Historical Society of Missouri, Columbia)

Dr. Ridge of Kansas City, played pieces for Blind Tom to imitate. He did so perfectly. Then Blind John, the mulatto boy, was called on. He played a Butterfly Gallop with his own variations. Blind Tom immediately sat down to the piano and reproduced the composition, variations and all. Blind Tom was then called upon and his composition was "Delta Kappa March." Blind Boone sat listening with rapt attention, knowing he would be called upon to reproduce it. He walked to the piano and played the march as accurately as Blind Tom. . . . Garth Hall was packed and the audience applauded enthusiastically, delighted that Columbia had a musical wonder equal to Blind Tom.

An account reported in the *Kansas City Times* of February 6, 1950, clearly favored Boone over Blind Tom. It stated that "When the excited crowd pushed forward to shake Blind Boone's hand, Blind Tom had disappeared backstage. He left town the next day and never again crossed Boone's path."

Although their careers have some similarities in the ability of each to imitate and in the nature of the programs they played, authorities disagree as to which of the two pianists was the more significant or talented. As stated in the *St. Louis Post-Dispatch* of October 30, 1927, Blind Boone, unlike Blind Tom, had a fully developed mentality and a philosophic grasp of the world as he knew it. Life to him was not a terrifying excursion in the dark. It was an experience made up of pleasant sounds and friendly touches.

After 1879, Boone's career was in the capable hands of John Lange Jr., a person of such substance and ability that his management of Blind Boone virtually assured the talented pianist's success. Lange, the second of sixteen children, was born October 4, 1840, in Harrisburg, Kentucky, the son of a freeman of Mexican and Creole parentage. John's mother, Louisa, and the children of the marriage belonged to James Shannon, who left Kentucky in 1849 to become president of the University of Missouri in Columbia. John Lange Sr. followed in about 1850 to be near his wife and children. He operated a dairy and grocery store with a butcher shop and was successful enough to own considerable real estate. He organized a Baptist church and school, which first met in his home. The school later moved to another site to become the Cummings Academy, and in 1898, it became the Frederick Douglass School. Lange was engaged in numerous philanthropic activities relating to Columbia's black schools and churches.

John Lange Jr. worked in his father's butcher shop after the Civil War and learned from his father the importance of contributing to the community. By the 1870s he had become a contractor; he built all but one of the roads in Boone County. He also built the first black Baptist Church. Although Lange later sacrificed his Columbia interests to

John Lange Jr. became a leader in the black community, using income from his position as a public works contractor to create employment, provide schools, and establish churches in Columbia. (State Historical Society of Missouri, Columbia)

serve as Boone's manager, he prospered in that role as well. Melissa Fuell described his home at 912 Park Avenue in Kansas City:

> The finely polished floors, the exquisite china paintings done by my milady's own hands, the brilliant gas and electric lights, shining through real cut glass chandeliers, revealing the extreme cleanliness of every corner. . . . A large "Chickering Grand" piano, occupies a prominent space in the reception hall, placed there for Boone's own pleasure, when he comes to Kansas City.

Lange eventually had assets valued at a quarter of a million dollars. His success disproved the predictions of his friends that "within six months you will be dead broke and will come into town pushing that boy in a wheelbarrow." The first few years did prove to be very difficult financially, and Lange's banker was thunderstruck four seasons later when he deposited a profit of $18,000.

Shortly after the Christmas concert of 1879, Lange gave Boone's mother a contract that guaranteed her ten dollars a month until Boone reached the age of twenty-one. At age twenty-one, Boone would join Lange as a full partner in the Blind Boone Concert Company. Meanwhile, Lange would cover all other expenses, including Boone's physical needs and tour expenses. Such a contract proved generous considering travel expenses; during the early years Lange and Boone frequently had little profit beyond the ten dollars sent each month to Boone's mother. Despite the need for greater profits, Lange never accepted an engagement if he believed the invitation came only because of sympathy. In establishing the Blind Boone Company, Lange developed a company motto: "Merit, not sympathy," to stress Boone's ability and dignity.

The peak years of Boone's touring career benefited not only from the managerial skills of John Lange but also from the opportunity he provided for Boone to further his musical training. Lange sent Boone to a professor at Christian College in Columbia, who gave him a few months of lessons in technique, introduced him to the music of Bach, Beethoven, and Brahms, and gave him valuable tips on phrasing and pedaling. The teacher was not identified by Fuell, but it may have been Anna Heuermann; we know that she did teach Boone at a later date.

Because Lange's mother had worked for James Shannon, a founder of Christian College, the Langes were able to arrange for Boone's lessons and for him to use the square piano at Christian College that had belonged to Shannon. About 1885, a Mr. Raisor, who served as a partner to Lange before Boone himself became a partner, arranged for additional training for Boone in Columbia with Mrs. M. R. Sampson of the Iowa State Teachers' College. Mrs. Sampson added twenty-five numbers to Boone's repertoire in two months and taught him the correct interpretation of the

classics. Boone received further training from Anna Heuermann of the Christian College music faculty from about
1893 to early 1896, when Miss Heuermann left the college.

As with many aspects of Boone's life, controversy remains concerning the date of his first professional concert.
Lange supposedly started Boone's professional career at
the Columbia courthouse on June 7, 1880. With tickets
priced at twenty-five cents each, the total receipts amounted
to a disappointing $7.00. However, the *Columbia Herald* of
June 17, 1880, reported:

> Columbia has a musical prodigy in a blind colored boy,
> who promises to become a formidable rival of the famous
> Blind Tom. Last week he gave a public entertainment at the
> court-house, which was well attended. His performances
> upon the piano were certainly remarkable and indicate ge-
> nius of no ordinary rank. Blind John, if properly brought
> before the public, would become a musical celebrity.

Actually Boone's professional career may have started before the June performance. A concert given January 18,
1880, at the St. Paul's Methodist Church in Jefferson City
was advertised in the January 8 *Lincoln Daily Tribune* as an
event of the Blind Boone Concert Company:

> Nature's Own Musician. He plays Liszt's Hungarian Rhap-
> sody, Beethoven's sonatas, operas, and many other grand
> selections to please and charm musical critics and teachers.
> He plays his cyclone imitation and a number of his own
> compositions and many of the every-day pieces familiar to
> the ears of all to entertain everybody. He gives imitations
> on his piano of the calliope, banjo, country fiddler, music
> box, guitar, fife and drum, morning train, and sings comic
> plantation and negro camp meeting songs, to make fun for
> old and young. The Blind Boone Company has secured the
> little 12 year old colored vocalist, Miss Stella. . . .

The Jefferson City concert appeared to be a professional engagement. The advertisement quoted the ticket prices (twenty-five cents for general admission, thirty-five cents for reserved seats) and reported that tickets were on sale at the Kennard and Riggs Drug Store in Jefferson City. The *Lincoln Daily Tribune* article of January 8, 1880, implied that Boone had already become well known.

The year 1880 and the concerts in Columbia and Jefferson City marked a turning point in Boone's life. After this time, with Lange as his manager, he could look forward to a successful career. Although there would be hardships and racism to face in touring, never again would he suffer the insecurity, humiliation, and cruel treatment from managers he experienced during his youth. He put the negative aspects of his career behind him, although much of lasting value had come from these years. His early association with both black and white acquaintances prepared him well for a career that transcended race, and his training and experience gave him the background necessary to bridge the gap between popular and classical music.

Chapter 4

The Touring Years

An act of nature gave an unexpected boost to Boone's touring career when a tornado struck Marshfield, Missouri, on April 18, 1880, killing 105 people. Lange read the newspaper account of this tornado to Boone, and Boone, who already had a cyclone imitation, immediately began composing his famous "Marshfield Tornado." According to the September 1969 issue of *Ragtimer*, Boone improvised the "Marshfield Tornado" on the spot as Lange read to him. He played this piece at every concert for at least the next thirty-five seasons, creating a remarkable impact on his audiences. In his 1979 article in *Missouri Life*, William Parrish gives a description of the realistic nature of Boone's composition:

> The piece began with chime-like sounds, as if calling the people to church; then followed a soft strain of sacred music, imitating the congregation singing an opening hymn. Then came a loud imitation of thunder, and fire bells giving the danger signal as lightening flashed across the imaginary sky. Finally, the storm died away, and Boone played softly, imitating water dripping from the eaves of the houses.

Later, Boone played his composition in Marshfield, "Playing with his wrists and elbows as well as with his fingers, and that audience went wild." The realism of the music reportedly panicked the Marshfield audience. Thinking another tornado was coming, people ran frantically out of the church while Lange tried to end the confusion by having Boone play "Dixie." Boone reportedly donated all proceeds from the concert toward rebuilding the town.

Boone's early tours experienced hard times and a shortage of funds. He was assisted by a banjo picker, a violinist, and the singer Stella May, but expenses forced Lange to discharge the violin and banjo players. In the winter of 1880 things became so bad that Lange had to send his wife, who was traveling with them, home to Kansas City. At one point, Lange offered himself and Boone for hire to a theatrical troupe for fifty dollars a month. This failed, and Lange sent Boone home temporarily until funds became available. The fact that Lange and Boone traveled by wagon and hauled the piano with them made their touring all the more expensive.

As Blind Boone's fame grew and he started performing widely, he received a growing number of favorable reviews. A review from a Cedar Rapids, Iowa, paper of January 1881 gave a vivid account of the music Boone played:

> Blind John was the center of attraction. Some of his performances are truly wonderful. He plays a tune called "The Shower," in which the listener can hear the pattering of the rain on the roof, and its dripping from the eaves . . . also the thunderclap and its retreating sound dying in the distance. On and above this could be heard a beautiful tune in all its parts. He performed a piece called the "Battle of Manassas," in which the fife and drum were distinctly heard, also the charge of soldiery and clang of small arms—the roar of the cannon both near and far off—the tramp of the recruits marching to the front. Above all this din of battle could be heard the measured cadences of "Hail Columbia." From his piano he can get banjo, guitar, and harp music in

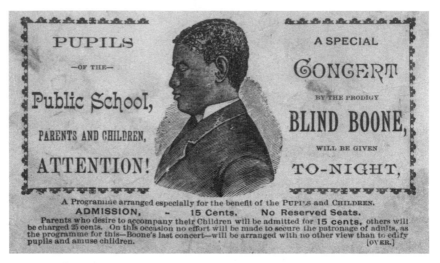

> PUPILS
> —OF THE—
> Public School,
> PARENTS AND CHILDREN,
> ATTENTION!
>
> A SPECIAL
> CONCERT
> BY THE PRODIGY
> BLIND BOONE,
> WILL BE GIVEN
> TO-NIGHT,
>
> A Programme arranged especially for the benefit of the PUPILS and CHILDREN.
> **ADMISSION,** - 15 Cents. **No Reserved Seats.**
> Parents who desire to accompany their Children will be admitted for 15 cents, others will
> be charged 25 cents. On this occasion no effort will be made to secure the patronage of adults, as
> the programme for this—Boone's last concert—will be arranged with no other view than to edify
> pupils and amuse children.　　　　　　　　　　　　　　　　　　　　　[OVER.]

Early in his career, Boone, pictured here as a young man, used performances in public schools to further his career. (Boone County
Historical Society, Columbia)

almost exact imitations. His business agent gave him a
mouth organ, and turning to the audience, he gave some
excellent viola music. He represented the various styles of
this music: that of the performer in the orchestra in a fash-
ionable theater, and that of the country dancing party, and
that of the plantation Negro on the Savannah.

According to Fuell, Boone performed in "Fort Wayne,
Iowa," on April 7, 1883, and another favorable review appeared in a local newspaper:

In many instances he excels Blind Tom, and when his youth
is considered we may look in a few years to see him in
every way far ahead of his rival for musical honors. His expression is excellent, his time good and his execution especially in octave passages, almost perfect. Particularly did he
exhibit his wonderful talent in "Rhapsodie No. 6," one
of Liszt's and considered one of the most difficult pieces
written.

Even with the success of the tours, life was sometimes hazardous and difficult. Melissa Fuell relates how fires added to the hardship of touring. In the fall of 1881, while Boone demonstrated pianos for the J. W. Jenkins & Sons Piano Company during the Kansas City fair, Lange left Boone for a few minutes to get a newspaper, and a fire broke out:

> Boone heard men moving out the instruments, and became very much alarmed. He told friends afterward that he would not run foolishly, for he did not know the way out, but he quieted himself and stayed at the same piano. He knew his friend, Mr. Lange, was sure to come for him, and should he move, he possibly would not find him.
>
> True to his trust, Mr. Lange rushed into the flames and smoke and recovered Boone just a few moments before the building collapsed.

Years later, Boone's company experienced another fire. In the fall of 1910 in Hay Springs, Nebraska, a fire spread from a barn to the hotel where the company was sleeping: "When Manager Lange saw one of his singers, Miss Jessie, hurrying with Boone down the stairs, he rushed into the rooms where the windows were already cracking and saved the baggage." The hotel burned completely, and the owner lost everything. A third fire occurred in Virden, Illinois, in 1914, caused by an overheated electric iron. Melissa Fuell saw the fire and quickly extinguished it.

Besides coping with fires, Boone experienced at least two train wrecks. One occurred in the spring of 1912 in Kansas as the result of a landslide. The other occurred in 1914 when a boxcar ahead of the passenger section overturned on the Illinois Central Branch from Carbondale to Metropolis.

Boone and Lange learned to handle troublemakers, a problem not uncommon for touring groups. They showed an inventive wit when dealing with disruptive youngsters:

Boone was often the center of attention as he waited for trains at railroad stations. He is pictured here in Clarksburg, Missouri. (State Historical Society of Missouri, Columbia)

In one village the Blind Boone Company found an exceptionally bad class of youngsters. They had been told that these youngsters would molest the patrons of shows so much by their noise, rock throwing, paper balls, etc., that the performers would either have to give them a free admittance or resort to the courts. . . .

Boone made friends with the boys, so he thought. . . . That night, however, they came for their usual disturbance. The manager met them at the door and told them that Boone wanted all the boys to go away and be quiet and tomorrow night he would let them in free. When the 'morrow came the company was in another town and the boys considered it a real good joke.

Certainly Lange and Boone experienced racial discrimination. When they traveled, the company often stayed in the homes of black citizens because no other accommodations were available. According to a 1904 story repeated in the *Warrensburg Star Journal* of March 20, 1981:

> Blind Boone, the well known Negro pianist and ex-Warrensburg resident, was denied admission to a Paola, Kansas, hotel recently. An old Negro woman took Boone's party in but would accept no pay for her hospitality. Boone learned the old woman had $350 mortgage on her home, and he paid it off, giving her a clear title.

Segregation had become constitutional during Boone's career as the result of the 1896 Supreme Court case of *Plessy v. Ferguson,* which upheld segregated facilities for blacks and whites traveling on trains. This opened the way for further segregation in hotels, schools, restaurants, theaters, and other facilities. States passed Jim Crow laws, requiring separation of the races, even demanding separate waiting rooms, restrooms, and drinking fountains. Accordingly, Boone's audiences were segregated. Boone frequently played two concerts in a city, one concert for whites and another for blacks. If both races attended the same concert, as in a 1893 concert in Warrensburg's Magnolia Opera House, blacks sat in a special section marked "reserved for colored people." In contrast to this, the *Mobile (Alabama) Register* of December 25, 1917, announced that a special section of seats would be set aside for whites for an upcoming Boone concert.

Throughout his career, Boone played in the small, sometimes isolated towns of Middle America. It was here, in particular, that his personal style of relating to audiences could be effective in opening doors to better racial understanding. He worked to overcome musical prejudice by combining the African American popular music with European classical numbers in the same concert. His very presence and success could encourage some degree of racial

Blind Boone with manager John Lange and Ruth Lange in front of the Langes' Kansas City home. Welvon Everett drove the touring car. Ruth Lange served as secretary for Boone's tours. (State Historical Society of Missouri, Columbia)

acceptance by whites, while serving as a role model for blacks in the audience.

Boone reached the peak of his career between 1885 and 1916. After May 18, 1885, when he became a full partner in the Blind Boone Concert Company, his income and his bookings increased greatly. By 1885, Boone and Lange together earned at least $150 to $200 a night, with good nights giving them $600 or more. Lange's wife once again traveled with the company, indicating an end to the hard times. Boone became so popular that the company toured for ten months a year from early September until late June. During these months, Boone had only Sundays off.

The Blind Boone Concert Company served as a training ground for several young singers. The first singer, Stella May, sang for thirteen seasons, until her voice failed. Another singer, Emma Smith, also experienced a voice failure.

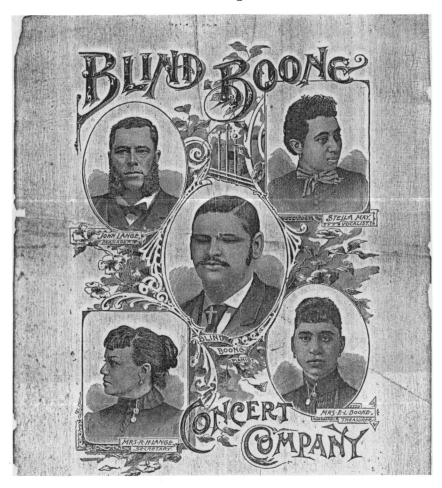

A typical handbill advertising the Blind Boone Concert Company pictured the members of the group. (Western Historical Manuscripts Collection–Columbia)

Smith sang for eleven years and did all the business correspondence for Lange, including keeping books and reporting to their headquarters in Kansas City. After she died on March 14, 1914, a statue was erected in her honor in Highland Cemetery in Kansas City. Another singer, Jessie Brosius, had acted as an assistant to Emma Smith for four seasons.

Melissa Fuell, who was to write Boone's biography, began singing with Boone at the age of seven. Other singers of less importance to the success of the Blind Boone Company included Black Patti, whose real name was Marie L. Jackson, of Sedalia. She studied with R. R. Dett at Oberlin, Ohio, and later became very popular on her own. Eliza Thompkins sang for one season, and Josephine Rivers sang for two seasons, later becoming a famous singer in the "Black Swan Company." Margaret Ward also sang with the company briefly.

The use of advance agents proved to be another factor that led to success for Boone. The agents traveled ahead of the company to schedule bookings, prepare for accommodations, and take care of advertising and railroad connections.

By 1915 Lange had used a series of white advance agents: Frank Thomas, Turner Gordon, W. G. Ketchum, L. W. Camp, L. F. Abbot, Bernard Foster, a Mr. Perkins, a Mr. Palmer, and James Shannon White. White was the grandson of the late James Shannon, once president of the University of Missouri, who had owned John Lange Jr. He worked for Lange for over eight years, gaining enough experience as advance agent to start his own lyceum. Palmer, the last agent before 1915, also started his own lyceum. Lange, realizing that white agents might move on for other opportunities, tried a revolutionary experiment by hiring a black agent, A. O. Coffin. Thus the Blind Boone Company proved to be a training ground for both singers and agents.

Everywhere Boone performed, he received glowing reviews, and full houses turned out to greet him. An article in the *Daily Nebraska State Journal* of January 9, 1888, shows a typical response to his concert. Boone gave a benefit performance for the ladies of the Alpha Society of the African-American Methodist Episcopal Church, St. Paul's Church; such benefit performances were typical of Boone's generosity. Stella May sang, and Boone sang while he played.

Boone played Schubert's "Serenade," popular songs, and imitations of instruments. According to the article:

> Professor Gibeault was called to the platform to test the power of the prodigy. When he struck a chord Boone would instantly name the keys that were sounded and was able to do the same thing with a fair degree of accuracy when a heavy chord or a long run had been played. Prof. Gibeault closed the test by executing a difficult selection from Rubinstein, which Boone immediately repeated with surprising precision. . . . The whole performance was interesting and well worth the liberal patronage given. . . . The entertainment has not been equalled in the city for some time.

Further recognition of Boone's ability came in a statement in *The Chicago Indicator* of May 26, 1888, that reviewed a performance: "Taking all things in consideration Blind Boone is one of the greatest and most remarkable pianists now living." Again, Boone correctly named the notes of chords and all the keys played. The *Indicator* reported that he showed his versatility by playing a varied program: "Marche Militaire" (Wollenhaupt), "Second Rhapsodie" (Liszt), "Mocking Bird," "Marching through Georgia," "Nearer, My God, to Thee," "Marshfield Cyclone," "Home Sweet Home" (Thalberg), "Last Hope" (Gottschalk), and a successful imitation of "Gavotte Rosita."

According to a review of another performance quoted by Melissa Fuell:

> Blind Boone, . . . one of the greatest phenomena of the musical world, entertained a good audience at the People's Church last night with his marvelous genius. There seemed absolutely no limit to his memory, while his technique was perfection itself. . . .
>
> The great feature was the execution of a composition depicting the tornado of Marshfield, which was grandly and

terribly realistic. Blind Boone will appear in another concert tonight. During the day he gave interesting exhibitions at Dyer's Music Hall and the High School.

Boone's Canadian tours reflect his success and appreciation outside the United States. A report of a concert appeared in an October 15, 1891, issue of the *Toronto World*:

> The remarkable pianist, Blind Boone, completed his engagement at the Auditorium last night. The audience was enthusiastic as ever. Each sat as if spellbound when the music sank to a scarcely perceptible whisper, but as the thundering crescendo filled the hall the applause shook the building, and as the merry waltz vibrated in the air a hundred toes lightly beat the floor. . . .
>
> Blind Boone has engaged with O. B. Sheppard for a four weeks tour in Canada next season for $12,000 clear of all expenses.

An article in the *Toronto Globe* of October 15, 1891, reported that "Blind Boone's audience has rapidly increased for the four entertainments given in this city and should he return to Toronto no doubt will insure him a full house." It is ironic that the height of Blind Boone's success in Canada in 1891 corresponded with the decline of Blind Tom, who, according to reports, was dying in an asylum in New York. When death finally came to Blind Tom on June 13, 1908, Boone remained at the peak of his career.

Boone's popularity in the town of his birth was reported in the *Miami (Missouri) News*: "Mertens Hall filled to capacity, hundreds turned away on Saturday. By far best entertainment in Miami for years." At this concert, as was typical of Boone concerts during his prime, many people stood outside, straining to hear as much as possible.

The nature of Boone's programs was described by Parrish in *Missouri Life*:

A typical Boone program would run about two hours without intermission. He always opened with a hymn—a favorite being "Nearer My God, to Thee"—which he would play with great embellishment. Several classical works from such composers as Chopin and Liszt would follow. Occasionally he would play imitations of other musical instruments on the keyboard.

A superb showman, Boone early adopted Blind Tom's ploy of inviting someone from the audience to come forward and perform a difficult number, which he would then repeat without missing a note. Many of these would be original or obscure compositions, and frequently the local performer would try to trick Boone by deliberately misplaying a passage. But the master of the keyboard would replay it exactly as he heard it, and then point out the mistakes and correct them—to the delight of his audience.

Boone would then move on to what were originally called "plantation songs," black melodies that had never been written down before, many he later notated. "Rare jewels of authentic Negro folk music," one ragtime musicologist has called them. Boone always liked to speak of this part of the program as "putting cookies on the lower shelf so that everyone can get at them."

His final concert piece was usually his famous "Marshfield Tornado."

One of the most fanciful descriptions of a Boone program comes from the *Howard County (Missouri) News* of March 10, 1904. Boone played to a large audience in the main auditorium and Sunday-school room of the Christian Church:

He carried the audience in a vaporous airship, lined with soft white clouds and lighted by a myriad of brilliant stars, high above sublunary things to a beautiful realm of music, sweeter than the enchanting notes of the siren's flute. They made the descension in a bird-shaped parachute and the sightless pilot placed them in the church as he found them, waved his magical wand, muttered a strange incantation and the spell was broken. . . . He has a peculiarity. His body is constantly in a swing motion which reminds one of the everbowing Gaston, the polite French character of comic-sheet fame.

If anything, Boone's ability seemed to increase after the turn of the century. The *Rising Sun,* a black Kansas City paper, stated on October 28, 1904, that Boone had performed at the opera house at Aberdeen, South Dakota:

> . . . this musician shows that wonderful gift of melody and harmony which is so often found in negro blood. He is full of music from his head to his feet. It is nothing short of marvelous that he has attained his reputation among such overwhelming obstacles.

A July 11, 1909, *Kansas City Post* article quoted by Fuell confirms his growth:

> . . . but there is none more unique than the Boone Company. Boone is a consummate actor; he interprets piano music by facial expression just the same as a singer does; every move of his expresses his musical feeling. He is not a mere "pounder" of the piano. . . . He also is a splendid interpreter of classic music, having studied with many of America's most prominent teachers, whose style he imitates minutely. . . .

Boone was also popular with his fellow performers. His relationship with James Scott of Carthage, one of the top ragtime composers, is shown in an article in the *Carthage Evening Press.* Boone was in Carthage for three performances, August 13, 14, and 15, 1904, according to the August 13 edition of the paper. The August 15 paper has a lively write-up of a reception and party given by Scott in

James Scott, a well-known
ragtime musician. (Courtesy
of Trebor Jay Tichenor)

his home for the whole Blind Boone Concert Company. A
delightful depiction of their warm relationship and of
Boone's ability also appears in the August 15 paper in an
article, "An Impromptu Musicale":

> A handful of people which grew to a throng as the enter-
> tainment continued occupied the Dumars music store Sat-
> urday morning when Blind Boone, Jimmie Scott, and
> Sousa's Band were the attractions. Boone chanced to call at
> the Dumars store to see his personal friend Jimmie Scott,
> the young colored man who enjoys a reputation as both
> composer and piano player. Mr. Scott played for Mr. Boone
> and in the course of his program did a new and certainly
> original stunt.
>
> A gramophone containing a Sousa band piece was
> turned on and Jimmie played a clever piano accompani-
> ment which really made good music. Boone was delighted

and before the selection ended said that he had to get his own hand in. He went to the piano and placing his hand on the treble made his nimble fingers fly over the keys in such a manner as to produce an accompaniment to the whole business which sounded like a piccolo. It seemed as if a whole orchestra was there and the audience was bewildered.

Both Boone and Scott followed with a number of selections both rag time and classical. Boone proved himself a rag time player equal to his unquestioned ability in the higher class of music.

The Blind Boone Concert Company had achieved fame and financial success by 1916. It had become so much in demand that it could not play every town requesting an appearance. By 1916, the company had toured the western and midwestern United States, Canada, and Mexico.

A summary by John Lange of the period from 1880 to 1915 was published in a *Columbia Missourian* article of June 3, 1924:

> Our record shows a continuous period of thirty-nine years of ten months each and six concerts a week, would make 8650 concerts that he has given.
>
> The distance we traveled would average 20 miles a day, or 216,000 miles traveled, while we slept in 8,250 beds.
>
> We paid to churches, halls and charity an average of $25 a day or a total of $216,000.

Because Boone had become so popular, piano factories willingly provided pianos for his use at concerts. Towns would also provide a piano for him, so that he no longer had to haul his own piano everywhere he went. However, Boone used his own pianos at home, and by 1915 he had worn out sixteen pianos.

Much of what we know about Blind Boone during the Lange years comes from the biography written by Melissa

Melissa Fuell sang with the Blind Boone Concert Company. She wrote an early biography of Boone, based on his recollections of his life up to 1915. (Boone County Historical Society, Columbia)

Fuell. Born in Warrensburg, Missouri, Fuell attended George R. Smith College at Sedalia briefly and graduated from the Lincoln Institute in Jefferson City, Missouri, with honors. After completing her education, she taught in Joplin, Missouri, for several years and later became a lecturer. She assisted the Boone Company singer Emma Smith, and Lange asked Fuell to sing for him when Smith left the company. Fuell soon became an assistant to Lange as well. By 1915 the company had become so successful that Lange determined to pay tribute to Boone by having Fuell write his biography. Fuell wrote a touching and informative, if somewhat quaint, book, of which they expected great things. A conclusion to the book written by an O. M. Shackelford, predicted that the work would be "in every public as well as private library in the country."

Few copies of the biography now remain. Sales must have been disappointing, but for those interested in Lange's concert company and in Boone, it is invaluable as the best source of Boone's own memories of his life to 1915.

The tenderness with which it is written shows the feelings of admiration Fuell had for Boone.

In addition to providing a wealth of information and honoring Boone, the biography successfully accomplished another special goal of the author. Fuell wanted the world to know the close relationship between Boone and Lange and how essential this relationship was to the company's success. She concludes:

> The two names, "Boone" and "Lange," are inseparable: Lange has lived for Boone; Boone has lived for Lange; Lange is true to Boone; Boone is true to Lange. Both are great big-hearted men and it is the author's chief desire to open the pages of their lives to the world, in order that men may honor them for what they have done.

The significance of the relationship between Boone and Lange, cemented by Boone's marriage to Lange's sister Eugenia in 1889, cannot be overemphasized. Lange was manager, friend, protector, provider, and confidant to Boone. Boone's career never fully recovered after Lange died in 1916. Later managers could not begin to be as effective. For roughly thirty-six years, Boone and Lange had traveled together from hardship to fame.

Blind Boone and John Lange Jr. "The most astute, dignified and successful manager of the race, and the greatest living musical prodigy, who have journeyed together in the Blind Boone Concert Company thirty-five years, a record unsurpassed or equaled by any other company, white or colored in America. Both philanthropic, generous and kind hearted to a degree, they are loved by their race throughout the length and breadth of America." *Kansas City Sun*, December 5, 1914. (State Historical Society of Missouri, Columbia)

Chapter 5

The Declining Years

The death of John Lange Jr. on July 21, 1916, signaled the end of an era for Blind Boone and foreshadowed the decline of the Blind Boone Concert Company. Lange died between seasons in his Kansas City home; he was seventy-five. His death robbed Boone of the only person he could truly trust and depend upon as manager. During Boone's last decade, he became sole owner of the Blind Boone Concert Company and acted as "head manager" himself for the rest of his career. However, John and Marguerite Day immediately assumed some of the managerial duties for him. Wayne B. Allen, owner of Allen Music Company in Columbia, assisted the Days and acted as Boone's manager after John Day's death in 1922 until the end of Boone's career.

In the last decade before Boone's own death in 1927, bookings became more difficult to obtain, and the company performed more and more in small towns and in churches and public schools. The tours concentrated on appearances in Missouri, Arkansas, Iowa, Kansas, Oklahoma, Nebraska, and Illinois. One notable exception to this pattern was a tour in the East during the 1919–1920 season. Boone played at Yale and Harvard and spent a month in Boston, a month in New York, and two weeks in Washington, D.C. This was his most extended tour, taking him into

Marguerite Day performed with the Blind Boone Concert Company and helped manage tours after John Lange died in 1916. (Courtesy of Trebor Jay Tichenor)

all of the large cities in the East and many small ones over an eighteen-month period. In an article in the July 16, 1920, *Columbia Missourian*, Boone expressed great satisfaction with the tour and the exposure it had brought him in new parts of the United States. He hoped to build on this base of popularity with future eastern tours. This never happened, however, and his later seasons were more limited.

By the end of his eastern tour, Boone had performed in forty-four states, as well as in Canada and Mexico. An interview in the *Columbia Missourian* of June 3, 1924, quotes him as stating that he had been to England, Scotland, and Wales. Later articles routinely repeat this, and descendants of Boone's relatives and friends express personal knowledge of such a tour but are unable to give specific dates. Neither Boone nor others ever recorded dates of a British tour or named places he performed, nor have publicity, reviews, or other information regarding such a tour come to light. The only newspaper reference found is a note in the

Fayette Democrat, reprinted in the *Columbia Missouri States-man* of November 17, 1892, claiming that Boone "... is now travelling in Europe displaying the instrumental skill with which he used to amuse Fayette folks. . . ." However, this source, which erroneously implies that Boone was from Fayette, may be mistaken. Nothing in the *Columbia Herald* or the *Missouri Statesman* is reported from July 1892 to July 1893 to verify the statement, while an item in the *Columbia Herald* of January 19, 1893, casts doubt on whether Boone could have been in Europe the previous November. The *Herald,* which commented occasionally on Boone's trips, reported on January 19, 1893, that:

> John Lange and his Blind Boone Company are taking a brief vacation in Columbia this week. Boone has been playing to splendid houses all through the northwest and goes west in a few days for another extended trip. Lange says he has all the dates booked he can possibly fill.

On February 2, 1893, the *Herald* reported that "Blind Boone and his company, under John Lange's energetic management, are on the road again. They will not return to Columbia for several months." Lack of information makes this subject another mystery of Boone's life.

In spite of the scarcity of bookings after Lange's death, Boone clearly had not lost his earlier genius, judging by the continued praise of his concerts. Mrs. Sam Davis of Warrensburg, who had been his childhood playmate and had taught him his first imitation, "Sultan Polka," remembered Boone in his later years. In a letter to the *Warrensburg Daily Star Journal* just before Boone's death, she wrote:

> As a concert pianist Blind Boone has often called for me when I happened to be in one of his audiences. He would ask me to come to the stage and play "Sultan Polka," his first musical accomplishment. . . . But I am not so adept in

the playing of "Sultan Polka" as I once was. At his last concert, five years ago (1922), in Mulvane (Kan.), for some years my home, he called for me. I responded and went to the stage, but I found I remembered only the first part of the composition I knew so well in my childhood. He hummed the remainder of it and tried to get me to go on, but neither my memory nor my fingers would serve me, so Blind Boone played the composition himself.

Wayne B. Allen had dealt with Lange and Boone as early as 1913 regarding the publication of some of Boone's music. About the time of Boone's eastern tour, Allen began booking some of Boone's concerts. Between 1920 and 1922, he worked with John Day in booking and managing tours. He became even more important to Boone after John Day was struck and killed by a taxicab in Chicago on June 25, 1922. Boone then relied solely on Allen, whose colorful account of how he became the pianist's manager is quoted by Madge Harrah in the September 1969 *Ragtimer*:

> I found out a man here in town [Columbia] had given Boone some papers to sign, under the guise of regular business, which turned out to be checks for large sums of money and deeds to much of Boone's property. I've never been so mad. I went to this man's office and I leveled my pistol at his heart. "You've known me all your life," I said, "And you know I mean what I say. Either you tear up those papers, or I drop you where you stand!" He tore up the papers. Then I went to Boone and said, "Don't sign another thing until I've read it first." So he made me his manager, and I booked him for seventeen hundred concerts over the next five years. When he became ill [1927], I cancelled fifty-seven concerts in Illinois alone.

Although Allen actually performed the duties of manager, Boone Company concert programs continued to list Boone as sole owner and manager.

Allen resorted to new ways to help make money as bookings became harder to obtain. He not only booked Boone more in public schools but tried to sell "School-O-Phones" for $125 each. Much of what we know about the years when Allen served as Boone's manager is in the Emma Azalia Hackley Collection in Detroit. Hackley, a well-known black concert singer, preserved the correspondence relating to Boone's touring in his later years. According to a pamphlet in this collection, Boone endorsed Allen's phonograph-like device for bringing music into the schoolroom:

> Blind Boone is a great lover of children and wished to bring about some provision for music in every schoolroom, and Boone endorsed it as the "World's greatest music instructor."

By the 1920s, Allen had to "sell" Boone to a public lured away from live acts by such new forms of entertainment as motion pictures, radio, and automobiles. The difficulty of booking the company led to the use of letters as a direct appeal, especially to schools and colleges. A letter from Allen to the president of Park College in 1923 states that "Boone has a beautiful new program including the 'Marshfield Tornado.' They say he is playing better than ever." A note at the bottom of the letter, which was returned to Allen, said simply, "Dear Sir, unable to arrange. Park College."

Although he could no longer attract such lucrative bookings as those of earlier years, Boone maintained a busy schedule in the 1920s, largely in Missouri and neighboring states. Correspondence between Boone and Allen from 1922 through 1926 reflects Allen's success in obtaining bookings in small towns. During an Iowa tour in 1923, Boone played four to six nights a week. A letter from Allen to the Booker T. Washington Theater in St. Louis, dated October 8, 1925, reports that Boone was unavailable for a week-long stand in St. Louis, as he was booked solid until Christmas. Again in 1926, correspondence shows Boone to be booked every night in a tour of Illinois, Oklahoma, and Kansas.

Obviously an industrious manager, Allen proved invaluable in the last five years of Boone's career. A letter from Boone to Allen, dated August 17, 1925, indicates that Boone leaned heavily on Allen: "I have turned everything over to you. To let you go your limit this entire season. With no interference by no one." Another document in a 1925 folder of the Hackley Collection shows that Allen had the power of attorney for Boone with all rights to Boone's contract with the QRS Company (a piano roll company) and full power to collect all royalties and sign and dispose of checks.

In spite of Allen's efforts, Boone faced financial and other hardships during his declining years. While he had routinely made over $100 a night in the years with Lange, by the 1920s he typically earned such amounts as $49.69, $55.00, or $68.92. Sometimes he accepted a flat sum of forty dollars a night. He began to offer Sunday concerts to increase his income and cut his expenses whenever possible. He even began sleeping overnight on trains. Even so, the long distances between engagements added greatly to the expense of touring.

Prejudice had again became a problem for the Boone Concert Company on his later tours. Small communities, unlike the cities of his peak years, sometimes resisted having a black in the town at all. A letter from the superintendent of the Ellinwood, Kansas, public schools shows how difficult it had become to tour:

> Should Blind Boone come to Ellinwood he may find some difficulty in finding accommodations. There are no Negroes here and the hotels are averse to taking in Negroes. I say this now . . . so the class will no way be held responsible for

his entertainment while he is here. There are any number of
Negroes in Great Bend. He might make connections with
them.

Boone also faced the problem of inclement Midwestern
winter weather. In a letter dictated by Boone to Allen, the
impact of bad weather on performing in small towns is
clear:

> Shortly after leaving Eldora this a.m. we came into another
> blizzard and this was the reason I was afraid of Iowa as it is
> a home of snow and the towns that accepted us are too
> small to depend on town trade. No town is much good in
> bad weather, less than 1,500 [dollars]. Last night it was $35
> and would have been better but snow prevented. This town
> is 900. Asking for 50 percent with a jump of 60 miles to our
> next date.

In addition to problems on the road, Boone had a rob-
bery in his Columbia home on August 29, 1922. As reported in the September 2, 1922, *Columbia Missourian*, a
prowler took jewelry from a purse in the dining room of
the Boone home. Items stolen included a 4⅓ carat blue-
white diamond ring in platinum setting with an estimated
value of $2,000 and another ring worth $350. Boone had
worn the diamond ring for thirty-two years.

In spite of such hardships and misfortunes, Boone remained publicly cheerful and optimistic. He expressed a
typically positive attitude in an interview with the *Columbia Missourian* on June 3, 1924:

> I was 60 years old May 17, yet I never tire of my work, or of
> practicing on the piano. I put in six hours in a working day,
> and I can still memorize twelve pages in two days. My
> memory is as good as ever.
>   I just closed my forty-fourth successful season a week or

so ago at Holton, Kansas. I started out in the fall of 1880 and have never missed a concert because of sickness.

In contrast to such positive attitudes, Boone sometimes expressed a desire to retire. On August 25, 1921, the *Columbia Missourian* reported that Boone "will leave October 1 for his 42nd and last concert tour." It was not his last tour, but again in the June 3, 1924, interview, Boone stated:

I am getting old, and I think that when I round out my forty-fifth season, I will quit. I may be like the others and give several farewell tours, for as has been demanded of the others, the people may insist that I come back again.

Boone made it clear in this interview that he had no sympathy for the new musical form of the day, jazz, as a replacement for ragtime, stating:

Jazz to me means something that tickles the feet and mind, and is a fad. Music is but conversation in tones, and I call jazz "foolish talk." Some of that kind of music has harmony, to be sure, but it is made to sell. Playing it, to me, is lost motion.

When the rigors of touring began to be too much for Boone, he concentrated more on performing opportunities in the Columbia area. On September 25, 1920, and again on September 2, 1922, the *Columbia Missourian* reported that Boone began his touring season with a concert at the Stephens College auditorium in Columbia. On September 28, 1920, he also made an appearance at the rehearsal of the University of Missouri marching band and played for them.

In an interview in the *Columbia Missourian* of January 5, 1926, Boone announced again his intention to retire. Recalling his classical career, he named Liszt, Chopin, and

Boone in his declining
years, wearing some of
the medals of which he
was so proud. (State His-
torical Society of Missouri,
Columbia)

Beethoven as his favorite composers. He concluded, "I am
going to retire and live in the happiness I have wrought
from others and in a final pursuit of those stray tones
which I have not yet found in my life."

Unlike earlier years, Boone was in Columbia for the New
Year and broadcast a New Year's Eve program on KFRU,
then the Stephens College radio station. The January 5,
1926, *Columbia Missourian* noted that the program engen-
dered more responses than any previous single program.
Another radio program on January 13 brought the same
enthusiastic response, showing that Boone's music still had
the ability to please. His busy month in Columbia included
a concert advertised in the January 6, 1926, *Columbia Missourian*, which announced in large letters the customary
motto, "Merit, Not Sympathy Wins!"

Boone gave his last concert, still assisted by Marguerite

Day, on May 31, 1927, in Virden, Illinois, ending with the traditional rendition of "Marshfield Tornado." While he was performing in Springfield, Illinois, just before the Virden concert, a doctor had recognized signs of "dropsy" (retention of fluid) and ordered Boone to go home. The report in the *Columbia Missourian* of June 2, 1927, cites ill health as the reason for the end of Boone's career. Another article, in the June 8 edition, says that Boone was home to stay, noting his "shortness of breath and increasing difficulty of getting about."

Even while Boone was resting at home, he planned future concerts as requests for his appearances continued. He continued to welcome visitors at his Columbia home and spent his last days in the midst of family and friends.

There are conflicting reports about Boone's activities just before his death, but it appears that he had intended to go to Hot Springs, Arkansas, for treatment. He rose early on the day of his death, October 4, 1927. He insisted that his nephew, Joe Hendrix, drive him to Warrensburg to visit his stepbrother, Samuel Hendrix, before the trip to Arkansas. One account speculates that he knew he was dying and wanted to be in Warrensburg, where his mother had died. Although some accounts place his death in Columbia or in Hot Springs, his death certificate confirms that he died of a heart attack in Warrensburg at the home of Samuel Hendrix at about 8:30 P.M. The author visited with Cozetta Brown of 408 Market Street in Warrensburg on August 19, 1985. Brown, a daughter of one of Boone's cousins, had become the owner of the property. She pointed out the spot in her backyard where Boone had died as he paused in Warrensburg on his way to Arkansas.

Boone's funeral and burial took place in Columbia on October 7, 1927, at 2 P.M. at the Baptist Church next to his home. The funeral proved to be a major event for Columbia's black community. Black children in particular flocked in large numbers to view his body. At his burial in the Columbia Cemetery on the rainy afternoon of October 7, Marguerite Day sang "I Done My Work." Blacks in Warrensburg paid tribute to Boone in a "resolution of respect," reported in the March 20, 1981, *Warrensburg Star Journal*:

> We need not try to speak to you of his wonderful achievements in life's work as a musician; history will take care of that and your children's children shall read of his great work, when we have gone from this earth. Brother Boone, who now lies upon the folding couch of death, has fought his way through life, step by step, having reached the pinnacle of fame, wrote his name not in clay but on the hearts of men and women.

Ironically, Boone's grave remained unmarked for the next forty-four years until 1971, when the citizens of Columbia decided to remedy the situation by erecting a marker.

Boone's will, written on October 2, 1924, named his wife, Eugenia, as executor. According to probate court records, Eugenia Boone swore on October 29, 1927, that she would faithfully execute the last will, pay all debts, and "render just accounts, and faithfully perform all things required by law touching such executrixship."

When the Boone County Probate Court made an appraisal of Boone's personal property, surprisingly little remained, although Boone had owned significant property both in Columbia and in Warrensburg. For example, in 1893, he had purchased a lot on the southeast corner of Walnut and Seventh Streets from one of Columbia's most prominent citizens, North Todd Gentry, for $5.00. This property was in a prime location close to the county courthouse, the center of activity in downtown Columbia at that time. The land's value certainly far exceeded $5.00. Possibly Gentry, who admired Boone, made a gift of the land to Boone, who paid a nominal fee to validate the "sale." In 1907 Boone bought a lot on Park Avenue, an unpretentious

Burial site of John and Eugenia Boone at the Columbia Cemetery, 30 East Broadway, Columbia, Missouri. (Black Archives of Mid-America, Inc., Kansas City)

street, for $725, a price better indicating land values in Columbia.

In his later years, Boone sold all real estate other than his home, using the home itself as collateral for frequent loans. Amounts borrowed include: $1,500 on October 31, 1918; $1,900 on August 22, 1921; $2,700 on June 22, 1925; $325 on December 20, 1925; and $500 on July 12, 1926.

The appraisal of Boone's estate listed his home at $4,000. Other assets of the estate included a Chickering piano at $500, a Swiss pocket watch studded with diamonds at $250, and a diamond scarf pin at $150. The only cash available came from the sale of the piano, along with a player piano and radio, all of which brought $250. Charges against the estate included $11.00 to the *Columbia Daily Tribune*, $12.50 to M. F. Thurston as administrator, $43.35 for court costs, $50.00 to the law firm of Clark, Boggs, and Peterson, and $50.00 to Sheriff Clyde Balew for serving the notice. This total of $117.35, when charged against the estate's cash of $250.00 from the sale of the piano, left Eugenia Boone with $132.65 and her home.

Claims filed against the estate totaling $3,137.17 were stricken from the files when the claimants never appeared to prove their accounts as required by law. These unpaid claims included $1,038 filed by Samuel Hendricks, $631.85 by the Allen Music Company, $882.32 by Marguerite Day, $539 by a Gustav Aldrich, and $46.00 by an O. H. Stark.

Probate court records contain the following statement in relation to Boone's other personal possessions:

> upon taking over of said estate on the 2nd day of May, 1928, the Executrix failed and refused to produce the watch and chain and the diamond scarf pin, and that all of the property that your petitioner was able to find and take possession of was the Chickering piano. Your petitioner states that since said date he has made diligent effort to find the watch and chain and the diamond scarf pin, but has been unable to do so.

The watch mentioned in the statement had become famous, as Boone had displayed it widely and newspaper articles had described it. Eugenia Boone clearly had possession of the watch at a later date, as she used it to pay a $50 promissory note. This watch, still a striking piece of jewelry, eventually became the property of George C. Miller, a Columbia attorney and businessman, who donated it to the Boone County Historical Society, where it remains. Although appraised at only $250 at the time of Boone's death, the watch had cost Boone $1,000 in the early 1900s. Michael M. Menser of Buchroeder's Jewelers in Columbia appraised the watch on May 21, 1983, at a value of $30,000, calling it an extremely rare collector's item.

The administration of the estate became more complicated when the probate court of Boone County declared

Boone's Chickering piano as it appears on display at the Boone County Historical Society. Manufactured especially for Boone in 1891, it was acquired by preservationists in 1960 and restored at a cost of $1,417.50. (Boone County Historical Society, Columbia)

Eugenia Boone of unsound mind on April 7, 1928. W. E. Smith became her guardian until his death on June 19, 1929, after which Lena R. Smith and M. F. Thurston acted as guardians until Eugenia Boone's death March 16, 1931. Eugenia Boone had borrowed money in 1928, using the Boone home as collateral, and the property was finally sold by her guardians on September 9, 1929, for $3,050 to Josephine Huggard Briscoe.

Of those possessions left after Boone's death, his Chickering piano became the most important as a symbol of his career. The piano had belonged to the Columbia Public Schools and remained at the Douglass School for many years. It now rests in the Boone County Historical Society museum. Boone had also owned a Steinway, an Estey, and a number of other pianos during his career. In addition, he owned an Edison Amburola phonograph and a Knabe piano with an automatic player that played music for Boone to imitate.

There has been much speculation concerning the disposition of the large amounts of money made by Boone during his career. While his generosity may account for some of the money spent, some acquaintances of Boone felt that he might also have been taken advantage of in his later years and that his estate may have been mismanaged. At any rate, what he left to his race and to the musical world has had far greater value than any tangible possessions.

Chapter 6

Boone as a Performer and Composer

Blind Boone's excellence as a performer, combined with his contributions as a composer, demonstrates his total importance to the music of his time. He drew upon his repertoire of popular coon songs, plantation melodies, religious songs, and ragtime as well as classical music in his performances. His wide repertoire allowed him to include both popular and classical selections in the same program, an ability that excited audiences about both realms of music. Not only did he bring both popular and classical styles to his audiences, but Boone also did much to bring black and white cultures closer together by the appeal he had as a musician for both groups.

Boone also played religious songs such as "Nearer, My God to Thee," "Holy City," "He Is My Friend," "Almost Persuaded," "Whiter Than Snow," and "You Can't Go to Gloria." As he frequently played in churches on his tours, religious songs were appropriate choices for his programs.

Boone gave special attention in his performances to southern plantation songs and coon songs, reflecting the social attitudes and popular culture of his day. The plantation, or "Ethiopian," melodies of the first half of the nineteenth century depicted slave life on plantations in a romanticized fashion. These songs, used very successfully on the minstrel stage, reached new heights of popularity in the 1890s. Boone's programs particularly stressed the work of Stephen Foster, who composed his first Ethiopian songs in 1845 and wrote the last of his great plantation melodies in 1869 with "Old Black Joe." Boone included, in addition to "Old Black Joe," "Massa's in the Cold, Cold Ground," "My Old Kentucky Home," "Swanee River," and "Carry Me Back to Old Virginny." Although Foster wrote his earlier plantation melodies in black dialect, he dropped the use of dialect with "Old Black Joe" to give the tune more universal appeal. Nevertheless, Boone continued to have his female singers perform these plantation songs in the authentic black style, using dialect, intensity of expression, and occasional hand clapping.

Boone's performances also relied heavily on coon songs. Coon songs used black dialect and depicted blacks in a flagrantly disparaging, though supposedly humorous, manner. The coon song rage of the 1890s carried over well into the twentieth century, and Boone continued to perform the songs throughout his career. He played a number of coon songs of his own composition, including "When I Meet Dat Coon To-night," "Melons Cool and Green," "Georgia Melon," "Dat Only Chicken Pie," "De Melon Season's Over," "Thanksgiving Turkey," "Dinah's Barbecue," and "Cause He's Tampering with My Chicken Coop Door." He wrote both music and words for these pieces, which reflected, as Edward Berlin wrote in John Hasse's *Ragtime,* the degrading caricatures of popular white concepts of blacks as stupid, lazy, and lovers of the stereotypical watermelon, possum, and chicken. The words from Boone's "Georgia Melon" illustrate the coon-song style of ridicule:

I
Dar's a many a kind of melon,
But dar's one I lob de bes'

It's from Geo'gia whar you gets um
    Always better dan de res'
Dar you gets em nice an' juicy
    Red clear up in de rin'
Sweet an' solid plump an' plunky
    Bless my soul but dey am fine

CHORUS

Dey am better dan de possum gravy
    Better dan de possum too
Watermelon, Watermelon
    You don' know how I lob you

II

Den away wid common melons
    Sot like tatters in a row
Raised like yeller Jersey punking
    War de sketters watch um grow
De mustard green am sugar sweet
    Dey say am might fine
But gim me dat good old Geo'gia melon
    Raised among de peanut vines

III

As far us dar's but one melon
    An' in Geo'gia dat one grows
She's a stripe from top to bottom
    Like a dandy darky's clothes
Ever sweet and ever juicy
    Watermelon, I lob you
Better dan de fines' pullets
    Better dan my sweetheart, Sue

IV

When I'm done an gon' to Glory
    'Fore I leave this earth below
I'll steal one vine from Geo'gia
    Whar dem big boss melons grow

When my wings am spread an' ready
An' dis darky says goodbye
Den I'll take my Geo'gia melon
An' I'll plant her in de sky

Boone, like other black performers, used coon songs in performances for both black and white audiences.

These and other songs that he presented were popular, but of greater importance was Boone's reflection of the evolution of popular culture in his use of ragtime. He probably began playing ragtime while he was still a student at the St. Louis School for the Blind, and he may also have played ragtime when he traveled with Mark Cromwell in the period before he met John Lange Jr. He continued to play it on the concert stage, with his "ragged" version of "Dixie" and with added syncopation and his own ragtime compositions, Southern Rag Medley Nos. 1 and 2.

Boone's own evolution from coon songs to ragtime reflects the musical trends of his time. Music historian Gilbert Chase sees a direct link between the earlier plantation and coon songs and the later use of syncopation in the coon songs of the 1880s that resulted in the full-fledged ragtime of the 1890s. Ragtime historian Edward Berlin, in *Ragtime: A Musical and Cultural History*, also notes that the coon song acquired the added label of "ragtime" in the 1890s and was "the earliest kind of popular song identified as ragtime." Boone serves as a prominent example of this development in popular culture. Perhaps his ability to reflect closely such popular trends and public response helps to account for his popularity.

Boone's numerous compositions, listed in the appendix, show his interest in a variety of forms and his love of music in its many styles. The best known of his compositions include two that are light classical pieces ("Woodland Murmurs" and "Sparkling Springs") and two genuine rags, Blind Boone's Southern Rag Medley Nos. 1 and 2.

Boone's success as a performer and composer of black and other popular music styles brought him to the attention of several companies that manufactured piano rolls. Information in the personal files of the musicologist Trebor J. Tichenor illustrates Boone's role in the field of recording, an industry described by Michael Montgomery, Trebor Jay Tichenor, and John Hasse in *Ragtime: Its History, Composers, and Music*. Boone began his recording career with the QRS Company of Chicago, a maker of piano rolls, in 1912. The company's name originated from its procedure for filing orders for piano rolls. When the orders, which were originally placed in the *Q* box in a cabinet, became too numerous for that space, additional orders were placed in the *R* pigeonhole, and eventually in the *S* space. The piano roll orders became known as "QRS orders" and provided the name for the company. The QRS contract, dated August 28, 1912, stipulated that he should play, among other pieces, "Dixie," "Swanee River," "Old Black Joe," "My Old Kentucky Home," "Massa's in the Cold, Cold Ground," "Camp Meeting Song No. 1," "Rag Medley No. 2," "Nearer, My God to Thee," "Woodland Murmurs," "Gavotte Chromatique," and "When You and I Were Young, Maggie." As a result of this contract, Boone produced one of the earliest hand-played QRS rolls.

According to Lee Roberts, who recorded the rolls, Boone became the first black pianist to make piano rolls. The 1912 contract obligated him to refrain from recording for any other company for a period of five years. It bound QRS to pay Boone's manager, Wayne B. Allen, a royalty of 10 percent of the net wholesale price of the rolls on a quarterly basis. Evidence suggests that QRS may not have paid Allen as much as the contract had guaranteed. Records show that on June 27, 1927, Allen threatened to file suit for "a true accounting of all sales made of certain Rolls recorded." However, Boone did receive royalties from QRS, some of which were paid as late as 1929, two years after his death. The only known royalty statement, dated August 1, 1924, would indicate that Boone received only a small income from royalties. The total amount for piano rolls sold on the quarterly statement came to $835.15. Boone's royalties, at 10 percent of the wholesale price of $417.58, came to a mere $41.76.

More important than the royalties is the fact that Boone successfully produced piano rolls of high quality for QRS. Some ten numbers, with one number per roll, still survive. Because QRS used the superior Melville Clark carbon method, the company could record Boone's playing more successfully than could other companies. According to Hasse:

> Clark devised a drum of paper that moved as the artist sat at the recording piano. The artist could hear the performance as it was being recorded. During the recording performance, pencil marks were made by eighty-eight tiny carbon markers as the piano keys were depressed. When the "recording" was finished, the result was a mark-up preliminary master roll. The next operation consisted of manually cutting out the marked spots with special die punches. After this step, the master roll was complete. Copying machinery could mass-produce many copies at a time from the master.

The surviving QRS piano rolls are valuable as a record of Boone's repertoire and of his playing style, but they do not accurately reflect his performing ability. QRS followed the practice, common to piano roll companies of the day, of editing, modifying, and embellishing the pieces with additional notes to add countermelodies, octaves, tremolos, and rapid chromatic runs to the existing recordings. As Hasse puts it, "Some rolls are so heavily . . . rearranged that they are called 'orchestral' arrangements—every note on the keyboard seems to play during the performance." Michael

Boxed piano rolls stacked above a piano player. (Courtesy of Trebor Jay Tichenor)

Montgomery, a historian of the QRS Company, described the recording process at the time of the early Blind Boone rolls:

> Obviously, any bad notes were also impressioned on the roll. Several women sitting at long tables then punched out this master roll with the carbon marks on it. Rolls were about 30–40 feet long. . . . Then an editor had to listen to the roll to find the mistakes, patch over the mistakes and punch in the right notes. Very few rolls, because of this editing process, have mistakes in them.

In 1918 Boone made some piano rolls for the Vocalstyle Company of Cincinnati, Ohio. George Hunt, the company scout, persuaded Boone to travel to the company headquarters for the recording. His contract promised a royalty of six cents for each roll sold; however, according to Michael Montgomery, Boone's Vocalstyle rolls were not recorded satisfactorily, as Vocalstyle did not use the superior Melville Clark carbon method. Instead, he reported: "A different process was used by VOCALSTYLE, the direct punch method. The paper travelled over a row of punches. You can imagine the terrific stress on the paper with these dies punching out the moving paper."

Because Vocalstyle lacked the sheet music necessary to correct the mistakes on the piano rolls, the company sent copies of the rolls to Allen for correction. Allen and Boone, who had little time to spare during the touring season, failed to complete the task over a period of months. Vocalstyle eventually destroyed the master copies.

Boone recorded for other companies as well. He went to Chicago in 1920 to record at the studios of the Imperial Player Roll Company. Although Boone made the trip in response to an invitation from the company, he discovered upon his arrival that the company meanwhile had hired another man. What followed became a sort of "play-off" as described by Allen and recorded in a September 1969 article by Madge Harrah in *Ragtimer*:

> After I became Boone's manager, we traveled together to Chicago where Boone was to audition for a piano-roll company. After we arrived, however, we found that the company had already hired a man from California. I left Boone downstairs and I went up where all the men were gathered and I said, "I don't care who you've hired, I have a man with me who can outplay anyone in the world!" So they said "Prove it!" and I said, "All right," and I wrote out a check to that company for a thousand dollars. Then I said, "If this man can't do everything I've claimed, this check is yours!" So I brought up Boone, and they brought in this man from California who had the longest fingers I've ever seen. A crowd had gathered by that time, and tension was running high. The Californian played first, for half-an-hour, his own composition, and he played well. When he finished at last, Boone applauded warmly, then walked unassisted

over to a second piano which no one had told him about but which he had located from hearing the over-tones. Without even sitting down, he said, "That was very good. This is the part that I liked best," and he whipped through the middle section without a flaw. That room went wild. The Californian shook my hand and said in a broken voice, "My God, I'd go to Hell and back for that man!" The next day Boone played the "Marshfield Tornado" for the rolls, but he went so fast and played so hard that he stripped the gears in the machine; so we came back to Missouri without a record of it, and now it's lost to the world.

Although attempts at recording the "Marshfield Tornado" failed, Boone did complete "Sparkling Springs." This piece, released later in the year, may have been the only piano roll by Boone sold by the Imperial Player Roll Company. There is no evidence that Boone ever received any payment from Imperial.

Boone also attempted to record 78-rpm lacquer discs for the Artophone Corporation of St. Louis, Missouri. He received an invitation from them in July 1925 to record for the Okeh Records in the Artophone studios. Any trace of the recordings that Boone may have made, however, has been lost.

Much of Boone's significance both as a performer and as a composer centers around his relation to ragtime. Although he is important in the ranks of early ragtime musicians, he stands apart from other ragtimers. He remained a musician of the classics as well as of rags. The impact of his early classical training led him to a career on the concert stage rather than to one as a performer of popular music only. According to the ragtime historians Rudi Blesh and Harriet Janis, Boone had the talent to join the ranks of such ragtime greats as Scott Joplin and Tom Turpin. Nevertheless, Boone, who knew Joplin and had some of the same goals as Joplin, belongs in a different category. Joplin did not play on the concert stage but specialized in the playing of ragtime in dance halls, nightclubs, and other such places of entertainment in which ragtime originated. Joplin wanted to make ragtime acceptable as legitimate music wherever it was played, not to take it to the concert stage.

Boone, comfortable in the white world, deliberately took ragtime from its lowly setting and put it on the concert stage to give it legitimacy. Both Joplin and Boone wanted to bring this form of black music to the white world and earn white appreciation for it. While they differed in setting and in method, they shared a common desire to tear down racial barriers and to serve as a link between black and white popular culture.

Boone's particular style in ragtime also set him apart from other ragtimers. He began performing ragtime before it became an established form in the 1890s, and he seems to have improvised ragging as part of his concerts. Ragtime historian Trebor Tichenor believes that Boone's early entrance into the field of ragtime is partly responsible for his different style. Boone began playing before Scott Joplin, Tom Turpin, Louis Chauvin, or James Scott. Because he began to perform his rag material before the ragtime era, he represents an important link between the black folk music of the plantation and coon songs to the early ragtime period. As a product of this early period, Boone's style was so peculiar that authorities disagree as to whether Boone was a typical ragtime composer. According to Tichenor, "this is more like folk music, more like what ragtime must have been at first. They are rare jewels of authentic Negro folk music."

Beyond his contributions to ragtime, Boone, as Terry Waldo has noted in *This Is Ragtime,* was the first performer to bring black spirituals to the concert stage. Again, his use of music from different sources to provide a "mix" of styles and types reflects both his versatility and varied background and experiences.

Boone is also a part of the evolution from ragtime to

blues. Both styles came from the same background, and, again, Boone became a pioneer in a new form. Certainly Edward Berlin sees Boone as a possible first in this evolution. He indicates in *Ragtime* that Boone's "Alabama-bound" chorus of his Rag Medley No. 2 (1909) may be the earliest publication of "boogie woogie," a form of blues.

Boone clearly contributed both as a performer and composer to the evolution of popular culture. Intimately connected with the very roots of ragtime, he symbolized this new music form, which appealed to multiracial audiences and which still gives a common sense of sharing to all who hear it.

Chapter 7

The Man and His Legacy

To understand Blind Boone fully, one must consider the person as well as the musician. In addition to the loss of his vision at a very early age, Boone experienced neglect, cruelty, and racial discrimination as a youth. He suffered the physical hardships of touring and the loss of John Lange Jr., who was his dear friend and a source of consolation and support. In spite of all this, Boone remained positive in his attitude. He maintained a spirit of kindness, generosity, geniality, loyalty, and closeness to friends and family. The *Warrensburg Daily Star Journal* of March 20, 1981, repeats a statement once made by Lange:

> I can truthfully say that he has not an enemy in the world. . . . Boone never sulks as did his predecessor Blind Tom, nor does he allow anyone around him to sulk. His favorite saying is "Just as you live, just so you die." He says time is too short and sweet to please the devil for even one moment. He is always charitable, and many times has authorized me when I see a deserving person in need to assist that person in his name.

Boone was successful in part because of his determination, enthusiasm, and hard work. He never doubted his own ability to succeed and always wanted to be an inspiration to others. His persistence at the Missouri School for the Blind in St. Louis paid off with opportunities that steered him toward a career in music, a course he had already anticipated. This same attitude triumphed over the hardships of one-night stands, long hours of travel, more hours of practicing, and eventually, illness. He continued with unabated optimism, planning for "the next season" right up to the time of his death.

Boone cut an impressive figure. As Fuell described him:

> [his] hands are short with delicately formed fingers, small feet, large head, with the same lines and shape of Beethoven's. He has a rich mulatto complexion and long black curly hair, very silken-looking and wavy. . . .

His size increased greatly as he grew older. Only five feet tall, Boone weighed less than 120 pounds at the start of his career. At the age of thirty, however, he weighed 225 pounds and gained to about 265 pounds at age forty-three. Most striking was the fact that his eyes had been sewn shut. Unable to walk without guidance, he frequently carried a child on his shoulder as a navigator.

Boone and others viewed his extraordinary memory as compensation for his childhood loss of sight. Indeed, his "flawless" memory made him appear so knowledgeable that some people considered him a walking encyclopedia. An article in the *Columbia Herald-Statesman* of February 12, 1915, reports that Boone kept a reader and translator as a way to study the lives of great musicians. He repeatedly expressed his delight in learning as much as possible about their lives and works.

Boone often had Lange or his wife read newspapers and other factual information to him. He reportedly knew every county in the United States and each state capital. He remembered every place where he had stayed and each

A rare photograph of young Boone with his wife, Eugenia, and his manager, John Lange. Eugenia was John Lange's sister and often read to Boone even before their marriage. (Black Archives of Mid-America, Inc., Kansas City)

person who contracted to play with his company. Madge Harrah quotes Wayne Allen, owner of the Allen Music Company in Columbia on Boone's phenomenal memory:

> There was an opera in town one week, and this star came into the store to buy some music. She saw Boone playing in the back room and said to me [Allen], "I met him in Kansas twenty-four years ago when I was playing in 'Uncle Tom's Cabin.' Let's see if he remembers my voice." Then she went back and spoke to him and asked, "Do you know who I am?" "Yes, of course," said Boone with a grin, "You're Little Eva."

Mary Paxton Keeley of Columbia told of an incident in which a construction worker who had met Boone in North Dakota came to a Boone concert in Columbia. The man shook Boone's hand, saying, "How are you Mr. Boone?" Boone recognized the voice and immediately replied, "Why Smith, you old rascal, are you building bridges in Missouri now?"

Similarly, a letter from T. H. Hamilton to Frank Smith repeated a story that was told by Hamilton's mother, Anna:

> After a concert at Fulton, many years after he had been her student . . . many members of the audience filed up on the stage to offer their congratulations. Mother deliberately did not speak before offering him her hand, but the moment he took her hand he said, "Why Mrs. Hamilton, I'm so glad you are here tonight."

Boone not only had an excellent memory, but he also reputedly could "see" things with his brain. According to the *Columbia Missourian* of August 25, 1921, Boone had actually described the appearance of a young woman. When the young woman brought a friend to him later, he exclaimed, "Oh this is a little red-headed girl, isn't it?" When a reporter came to Boone's home in 1924, Boone demonstrated his ability to "see things with his mind," as reported in the June 3, 1924, *Columbia Missourian*:

> He then told the exact weight and height, complexion and general characteristics of his interviewer. It was not hokuspokus. No one had said a word to him from the outside. His description was too nearly accurate to be guesswork. He seemed pleased when told that his "picture" was almost perfect.

Mrs. Corene Turner of Columbia, who knew Boone, recalled that she wore a silk dress with a pink flower on it; Boone felt the dress and could tell the color of the flower. Yet another source recalled how Boone could put his hand on a child's head and tell the child's age.

Boone's great talent and warm, happy personality won him many friends wherever he went. As several sources reported, "He never lost a friend. No one ever heard him make a bitter or cynical remark, and he was apparently incapable of doing an unkind act." According to Fuell, he won acclaim from such celebrities as President Hayes; the composers Paderewski and Rachmaninoff; Governors Crittenden, Francis, and Stephens; and numerous senators.

At each town Boone visited, children flocked to him. They especially enjoyed hearing stories about Boone's youth and examining his unusual gold pocket watch. The watch understandably fascinated children, and it was a constant part of Boone's wardrobe. An eighteen-karat-gold tricolored pocket watch, its movement included a perpetual calendar showing the day, date, month, and phase of the moon. The backside of the case displayed a horse's head design surrounded by a horseshoe with seven diamonds set into the case.

Frequently Boone would ask children their names and invite them to attend his concert as his guests. At the concert, Boone would lead these youths into the concert hall, where he would call out their names to see how many of them had accepted his invitation.

Boone loved the companionship of belonging to fraternal organizations. Melissa Fuell tells us that he was a thirty-second-degree Scottish Rite Mason, a Royal Patron of the Eastern Star, a Patriarch of Odd Fellows, a Grand Prelate of the Knights of Pythias, and a Grand Chaplain of the United Brothers of Friendship. He was also a member of the Eastern Star, V.B.F., of the Elks, and of the Mosaic Templars.

Boone's immediate family consisted only of his wife and his mother. His mother, who died on January 9, 1901, had lived on a four-acre estate in Warrensburg that Boone had bought for her. Boone saw to it that his five stepbrothers kept the old home in the family. He instructed them to keep the home neat "out of deepest respect for her loving

Blind Boone's watch, photographed by Mary Paxton Keeley. (State Historical Society of Missouri, Columbia)

memory." Boone also maintained a close relationship with his wife. An article in the Henry Fike papers in the Western Historical Manuscripts Collection describes his anxiousness to be near his wife when she became ill:

> Blind Boone, the negro pianist, went from Kansas City to Columbia, Mo., in a special train yesterday, over the Wabash. While playing in Nebraska he had received word that his wife had been taken suddenly ill. He hurriedly canceled his engagements and took the first train for home. Arriving here [Kansas City] yesterday morning, he discovered that he was too late for the 10 o'clock train over the Wabash office, and rather than wait until evening he went to the Wabash office, laid $200 on the counter and called for a special train. One coach and an engine was hastily provided, and in a few minutes the way was being cleared for the Blind Boone special as it raced to Columbia, taking the negro to the bedside of his sick wife.

Boone and Eugenia re-
mained devoted until
Boone's death in 1927.
(State Historical Society
of Missouri, Columbia)

Although Boone traveled about ten months of each year, he
regarded Columbia as his home and valued the time spent
there with his family and friends. The Columbia of Boone's
lifetime was a rapidly growing town, according to Columbia historian John Crighton. Its population increased
through annexation from 3,326 in 1880 to 5,651 by 1900. In
1904, Columbia voters authorized the city to spend a hundred thousand dollars to construct a water works and electric light plant. Broadway was paved with brick from Sixth
to Tenth Streets in April of 1906, and that same year, Columbia added sewers and a fire department. The streets in

black neighborhoods, however, remained dirt roads, and most black families still had outhouses in place of plumbing and sewers. It was not until the 1950s that Columbia installed sewers, paved the streets, and provided public housing in the black community.

Churches were an important source of support for the black community in Columbia, serving as social as well as religious centers. Blacks in the white-dominated Baptist and Methodist Episcopal churches of Columbia formed their own African Union Church in 1865. The Methodists withdrew, leading the Baptists to organize a black Baptist Church and school in 1866 in the home of John Lange Sr. The congregation moved from the Lange home to the building intended for the African Union Church until their own church was completed in 1873 at Fifth and Cherry Streets. Boone gave generously to this church as well as to the Second Baptist Church at 407 East Broadway and the St. Paul African-American Episcopal Church. His career was closely tied to black churches not only through his philanthropy but also through his use of black church buildings for performances.

Boone's generosity included gifts and loans to several schools and churches in Columbia. This included a loan of two thousand dollars to Christian College in 1890, due in twelve months at 6 percent interest. Boone also lent three thousand dollars toward the construction of the Second Baptist Church, which was completed in 1894. As the result of these gifts and loans, he declared that he put more roofs on Columbia churches than anyone else.

Blind Boone moved into his permanent home in Columbia after his marriage in 1889 to Eugenia Lange. The house was located on the "Flat Branch," a creek made famous in his Southern Rag Medley No. 2: *Strains from Flat Branch.* Built in 1880, the house extended south from Walnut Street along Fourth Street. Located just north of the Second Baptist

Blind Boone in his Columbia home. (Western Historical Manuscripts Collection–Columbia)

Church at Fourth and Broadway, the home later became
the Warren Funeral Chapel. A number of structures in the
area—including Boone's home, which Columbia leaders
hope to restore for a museum; the Second Baptist Church at
407 East Broadway; the Second Christian Church at 401
North Fifth; St. Paul Church at 501 Park; and Douglass
School at 310 North Providence Road—were all placed on
the National Register of Historic Places on September 4,
1980, as sites showing significant achievement in Columbia's black community. All of these institutions profited
from the generosity of Blind Boone, who gave benefit concerts to further their projects. These five buildings, so important to the black community, became symbolically
bonded to Boone's career. As stated in the nomination form
for their placement in the National Register: "Blind Boone

Blind Boone home now. (John William Boone Heritage Foundation; photographed by Greg Olson)

lives on as an example of a dream of fulfillment that can come true for the black community."

Columbia, as Boone's hometown, has honored the musician in several ways. In the 1950s, when the public housing project replaced the substandard housing in the black community, the area was dedicated as the John W. Boone Housing Project with the Blind Boone Recreational Center as a major gathering place for black youths. In 1961, the Blind Boone Memorial Foundation presented a concert using Boone's own 1891 Chickering piano. Frequent concerts since that time continue to honor him, and his famous piano forms the centerpiece of a special display at the Walters–Boone County Historical Museum. When Columbia and Boone County celebrated the Sesquicentennial of Missouri's statehood in 1971, contributions finally made it possible to place a tombstone on the graves of Boone and his wife, Eugenia, buried by his side. The sesquicentennial history, *A Boone County Album,* included a chapter on Boone. Most recently, measures to make a museum of Boone's home bring the prospect of a permanent focus for the celebration of his career.

Boone's love of people and love of life carried over into his career, enabling him to respond to and please audiences. Reviews and testimonials repeatedly cite his love of music and his desire to pass that love on to others. Even his wide and varied repertoire may have been the result of this desire to offer something for everyone. He routinely played classical music in the first part of his program and popular music later in the program. According to the ragtime historian, Terry Waldo:

> Boone would not only play the standard classics of Liszt, Chopin, and Beethoven, but he would also include raggy Negro music. After the first intermission, he would say, "Now I'll put the cookies on the lower shelf where everyone can reach them," and he would launch into one of his Negro folk medleys.

Boone's musical ability was widely recognized. Reviewers consistently testified to his proficiency and to his remarkable ability to play back what he had heard. His incredible memory constantly impressed audiences.

Boone was a product of his experience, his training, and his time. He experienced both black and white friendships throughout his life. He loved the white man's classical music in the European tradition as well as his own black folk music in the African tradition. In this sense, he truly bridged the gap between classical and popular traditions and between black and white cultures. Waldo compared Boone to the virtuoso pianist and composer Louis Moreau Gottschalk, who drew on the New Orleans locale for such compositions as "The Banjo" and "Bamboula," which pointed the way to an awakening nationalism.

John William ("Blind") Boone is another nineteenth century pianist who is important in the same respect as Gottschalk. This black artist from Missouri was the first performer to bring the Negro spiritual to the concert stage.

Because of these unique features of Boone's life, he played an important role in the evolution of popular culture. Boone, as a mulatto, was himself a racial and cultural mix. Ragtime, as a new musical form, became the same sort of musical mix. Early rag or classical rag, which Boone played and composed, carried African American traditions into the white world. Boone, because of his classical training, had a natural affinity for this form, which combined fixed notation and the European background with "ragging." Boone's own evolution from plantation melodies and coon songs to ragtime truly reflects the evolution of popular music itself. His achievements, resulting from significant changes in American music and society, helped create new musical forms for the benefit of all.

Appendix

List of John William Boone Compositions and Transcriptions

Plantation Songs, Folk Songs, Coon Songs, and Spirituals

" 'Cause He's Tampering with My Chicken Coop Door."
"Christening of Abe Jones' Baby."
"Cleo (Waltz Song)." Philadelphia: Ditson, 1886.
"Dat Mornin' in de Sky." Kansas City: Carl Hoffman, 1899.
"Dat Only Chicken Pie."
"De Melon Season's Over."
"Dinah's Barbecue (Song and Break Down)." St. Louis: Kunkel, 1893.
"Do You Call That Religion?"
"Georgia Melon." Columbia: W. B. Allen, 1908.
"Good News."
"Humorous Song."
"Melons Cool and Green (Plantation Song and Chorus)." St. Louis: Drumheller-Thiebes, 1894.
"No Time for Argument."
"Now Let Me Fly."
"Open de Window, Let de Dove Come In."
"Signs of the Times."

"Thanksgiving Turkey."

"That Little German Band." St. Louis: Kunkel, 1894.

"Whar Shill We Go When de Great Day Comes." New York: Willis Woodward, 1892.

"When I Meet Dat Coon To-night." New York: Willis Woodward, 1892.

"You Can't Go to Gloria." St. Louis: Kunkel, 1893.

"You Can't Make It Win at de Gate."

Ragtime Compositions

Blind Boone's Southern Rag Medley No. 1: *Strains from the Alley* (urban material). Columbia: W. B. Allen, 1908.
"I Got a Chicken on My Back."
"Oh, No Babe!"
"Make Me a Pallet on the Floor."
"I Certainly Does Love Dat Yellow Man."
"Dat Nigger Got Lucky at Last."

Blind Boone's Southern Rag Medley No. 2: *Strains from Flat Branch* (rural material). Columbia: W. B. Allen, 1909.
"Carrie's Gone to Kansas City."
"I'm Alabama Bound."
"So They Say."
"Oh! Honey Ain't You Sorry."

Songs and Classical Piano Music

"Aurora Waltz." Columbia: W. B. Allen, 1907.

"Camp Meeting Song No. 1." [Southern Camp Meeting Songs Interpreted by Boone.]
"Judgment Will Find You Soon."
"As Long as I Can Feel the Spirit."
"Open the Window, Let the Dove Come In."
"Home in the New Jerusalem."

"I Have a Heaven in the Promised Land."

"Canoeing (Boat Song)."

"Caprice de Concert No. 1." St. Louis: Kunkel, 1893.

"Caprice de Concert No. 2." St. Louis: Kunkel, 1898.

"Caprice de Concert No. 3 (Danse des Negres)." St. Louis: Kunkel, 1902.

"Caprice de Concert No. 4." St. Louis: Kunkel.

    1. "Nicodemus."

    2. "Granny Will Your Dog Bite?"

    3. "Old Steve Runyan."

"Child's Picnic, Introducing

    1. Marching around the Levy

    2. King William Was King James' Son

    3. Run Liza Jane."

"Danse des Negres, Caprice de Concert." St. Louis: Kunkel, 1902.

"Dixie: Piano Fantasy."

"Echoes of the Forest."

"Eve to Dawn (Serenade)."

"Gavotte Chromatique."

"Grand Tarantelle de Concert (Enchantment-Tarantella-Morceau de Concert)."

"Grand Valse Brilliante in E-flat."

"Grand Valse de Concert." Kansas City: J. W. Jenkins, 1893.

"The Humming Bird: Morceau de Salon." Boston: O. Ditson, 1886.

"Josephine Polka." Cincinnati: John Church, 1891.

"King Chanticleer."

"Last Dream (Waltz)." Columbia: W. B. Allen, 1909.

"London Bridge Is Falling Down."

"Love Feast (Waltz)." Columbia: W. B. Allen, 1913.

"Marshfield Tornado."

"Old Folks at Home (Grand Fantasie)." St. Louis: Kunkel, 1894.

"Our Boys Will Shine Tonight."

"Serenade (Song without Words)." Boston: O. Ditson, 1887.

"The Shower."

"Sparks (Galop de Concert) (Piano Duet)." St. Louis: Kunkel, 1894.

"Sparks (Galop de Concert) (Piano Solo)." St. Louis: Kunkel, 1894.

"The Spring: Reverie for Piano." Boston: O. Ditson, 1885.

"Sultan Polka."

"To Thee Edna (Song without Words)."

"Whippoorwill: Romance for Pianoforte." Boston: O. Ditson, 1891.

"Woodland Murmurs: A Spinning Song." Boston: O. Ditson, 1888.

Old Favorites with Variations by Boone

"Annie Laurie."

"Believe Me, of All Those Endearing Young Charms."

"Bonnie Sweet Bessie."

"Butterfly Gallop."

"Carnival of Venice."

"Dixie."

"Home, Sweet Home."

"Last Hope."

"Last Rose of Summer."

"Listen to the Mocking Bird."

"When You and I Were Young, Maggie."

Boone's Transcriptions of Plantation Songs

"Carry Me Back to Old Virginia."

"Massa's in the Cold, Cold Ground."

"My Old Kentucky Home."

"Old Black Joe."

"Swanee River."

Miscellaneous Performance Favorites

"Drummer Boy."
"Gospel Train."
"Imitation of Banjo."
"Imitation of Country Man Tuning Fiddle."
"Imitation of Fife and Drum."
"Imitation of In-coming Train."
"Imitation of Music Box."
"Marching through Georgia."
"The Mocking Bird."
"Peek-a-boo."

For More Reading

America's Black Musical Heritage, by Tilford Brooks (New Jersey: Prentice-Hall, 1984), covers all American black music from its roots to the present day. At the end of the book, useful sections, including lists of compositions and of recordings of compositions by composers cited in the study, and an extensive bibliography, add to the value of the work.

Black Music in America, by John Rublowsky (New York: Basic Books, 1971), traces the black musical heritage from its roots in Africa through the slave-trade era and through American history, culminating with the jazz of the 1950s. Treatment of ragtime is limited, but black music as a whole is well covered. Includes a selected bibliography.

Blind Boone: His Early Life and His Achievements, by Melissa Fuell (Kansas City: Burton Publishing Company, 1915), is the first biography written about Blind Boone. It covers Boone's life from birth to about 1915. Much of what we know about Blind Boone's youth and early career comes from this book.

"Blind Boone's Ragtime," by William Parrish, *Missouri Life* (November–December 1979), 17–23. This article discusses the evolution of ragtime music, Blind Boone's life and career, and his legacy.

A Boone County Album, ed. by James Darrough (Columbia: The Columbia/Boone County Sesquicentennial Commission, 1971), though not intended to be a comprehensive history of Boone County, does contain separate chapters on some of the more notable citizens, places, and events of the county. It includes a chapter on Blind Boone, featuring pictures of Boone, his piano, his watch, and his home on Fourth Street.

The Continuing Enslavement of Blind Tom, The Black Pianist-Composer (1865–1887), Book 2, by Geneva Southall (Minneapolis: Challenge Productions, 1983), is the best-known work on the life and career of Blind Tom.

King of Ragtime: Scott Joplin and His Era, by Edward A. Berlin (New York: Oxford University Press, 1994), is a comprehensive work on the life, music, and legacy of Scott Joplin. Carefully researched, it places Joplin in the setting of the time. An extensive bibliography is included.

"Life and Career of Blind Boone," by Jack Alan Batterson (Master's thesis, University of Missouri–Columbia, 1986), is based on extensive research in books, newspapers, and periodicals to locate articles and reviews relating to Blind Boone's life and musical achievement. It analyzes his stature as a composer and performer and includes listings of articles in Midwestern and other newspapers describing Boone's concerts, listings of books that discuss his place in musical history, and information relating to commemorations of

Boone's work. The thesis may be borrowed from Ellis Library, University of Missouri–Columbia.

The Music of Black Americans: A History, 3d ed., by Eileen Southern (New York: Norton, 1997), is a comprehensive coverage of black music from the early roots to the contemporary scene. Ragtime is mentioned as one of several precursors of jazz. A generous bibliography and discography at the end of this book leads readers to further sources for research.

Negro Folk Music, U.S.A., by Harold Courlander (New York: Columbia University Press, 1969), puts African American folk music in the larger framework of cultural continuity and its relation to other movements, asserting that it is the largest body of genuine folk music still alive in the United States. It discusses various musical styles, settings, and instruments and includes an extensive bibliography by musical styles and a collection of musical scores.

Rags and Ragtime: A Musical History, by David A. Jasen and Trebor Jay Tichenor (New York: Seabury Press, 1978), includes chapters such as "Ragtime as a Form and a Fad," "Early Ragtime: 1897–1905," "The Joplin Tradition," "Popular Ragtime: 1906–1912," "Advanced Ragtime: 1913–1917," "Novelty Ragtime," "Stride Ragtime," "Jelly Roll Morton," and "The Ragtime Revival: 1941–1978." The appendix includes a list of the more important ragtime composers with information about their music and recordings.

Ragtime: A Musical and Cultural History, by Edward A. Berlin (Berkeley and Los Angeles: University of California Press, 1980), is a meticulous study of ragtime, based on over a thousand compositions and a well-

documented history of what ragtime was and its social
significance. It surveys attitudes expressed about ragtime by its contemporaries and how these attitudes
have changed since the ragtime era. Piano ragtime is
subdivided into several stylistic categories. It includes
informative footnotes and has an outstanding bibliography, organized by sources before 1930 and those
after that date.

Ragtime: Its History, Composers, and Music, ed. John Ed-
wards Hasse (New York: Schirmer Books, Macmil-
lan, 1985), includes chapters written by the leading
American experts, such as Edward A. Berlin, Michael
Montgomery, Max Morath, Addison W. Reed, Guy
Waterman, Joseph R. Scotti, James Dapogny, Frank J.
Gillis, Roland Nadeau, and Thornton Hagert. The
book also includes an outstanding list of books and articles about ragtime, a large discography, and a long
list of ragtime folios and methods for a variety of instruments. It also provides a checklist of music mentioned in the book.

They All Played Ragtime: The True Story of an American Music,
by Rudi Blesh and Harriet Janis (New York: Alfred A.
Knopf, 1950), one of the earliest histories of ragtime,
gives thorough coverage of all significant individuals,
black and white. It gives special attention to Missouri
in the coverage of geographic areas. Appendices list
ragtime compositions, player-piano rolls, cylinder phonograph records, and selected ragtime records. It has
no bibliography.

This Is Ragtime, by Terry Waldo (New York: Hawthorn
Books, 1976), is a thorough and outstanding study of
all aspects of ragtime, from its roots to the 1970s, and
contains a selected discography and bibliography.

Index

About the Author

Jack A. Batterson, a native of Columbia, Missouri, earned his bachelor of arts and master of arts degrees in music history at the University of Missouri–Columbia. He then attended the University of Indiana at Bloomington for his master's in library science and presently works in technical services at Ellis Library at the University of Missouri–Columbia. He serves on the Board of Directors of the Blind Boone Foundation, a group directing efforts to make Boone's home a permanent museum. He continues his interest in music, playing the clarinet in local bands. Mr. Batterson and his wife, Mary, live in Columbia.